Holiday Hoopla: Multicultural Celebrations

by Kathy Darling

illustrated by Marilynn G. Barr

Publisher: Roberta Suid
Copy Editor: Carol Whiteley
Design and Production: Susan Pinkerton
Cover Design: David Hale

Other books by the author in the Holiday Hoopla series:
Songs and Finger Plays; Flannel Board Fun;
Plays, Parades, Parties; and *Multicultural Folk Tales*

Monday Morning is a registered trademark of
Monday Morning Books, Inc.

ISBN 1-878279-73-4

Printed in the United States of America
9 8 7 6 5 4 3 2

Contents

Introduction

One certain way to learn something new is to put yourself in another person's shoes for a while; while doing this, you're also likely to find out how much the two of you have in common. Using the activities in *Holiday Hoopla: Multicultural Celebrations*, you and your students will be able to do both of these things. The activities will help you take a new look at familiar holidays, as well as learn about holidays that are less well known to you. And they will allow you and your students to see that many types of celebrations and ideas are common to people everywhere.

The book offers projects based on a wide variety of holiday customs from around the world, from Japan's Hina-matsuri to India's Diwali Festival to Northern European Christmas traditions. By taking part in these activities, your class may come to realize that other children, though they live far away, share many of the same beliefs that they do, even if they practice them in a slightly different way. The children will find that rites of the harvest, celebrations of life, and recognition of the family are universal traditions as they discover the common threads that bind all people.

Holiday Hoopla: Multicultural Celebrations has attempted to preserve the most important aspect of each culture's traditions while adapting them for classroom, day care, and home use. While not a complete guide to the cultural festivities that take place around the world, the book offers an introduction to many of these sometimes complex, changing traditions, and encourages you to expand on the information provided by talking with natives of the countries highlighted and calling on knowledgeable people and resources of your own. Your local library can be an excellent source of music to accompany classroom celebrations, and a globe or map to locate countries whose traditions you are studying will be invaluable.

To help you and your students experience many of the facets of holiday customs, the book includes a variety of projects, including crafts, games, songs, and snack ideas. Some projects, for example, those in which small objects such as buttons or sequins are involved, will require close supervision, and some will ask that you prepare materials ahead of time. But most activities will require only readily available materials and can be done by the children with minimal guidance from you.

Holiday Hoopla: Multicultural Celebrations aims to offer you a well-rounded program that brings fun, festivity, and understanding to multicultural experiences around the globe. A companion book, *Holiday Hoopla: Multicultural Folk Tales*, can serve as a complement to this program.

The Chinese Mid-autumn, or Moon, Festival is the traditional time of thanksgiving for abundant harvests. On the night of this festival the moon is full, and some call it the moon's birthday. Special moon cakes are baked from pale yellow flour and served on a plate surrounded by four dishes of different fruits presented in rings or rounds.

Moon Cakes

This simple version of the recipe uses easy-to-find ingredients.

Ingredients:
Individual-size shortcakes or baked pie crusts, vanilla pudding, crushed almonds, raisins, bits of chocolate, sugar, whipped topping (optional)

Preparation:
Mix the almonds, raisins, and chocolate with a bit of sugar. Spoon into the vanilla pudding.

Activity:
Give each child a shortcake (a "moon cake") on a small paper plate. Let the children spoon a bit of the pudding mixture into the center of their cake. Add whipped topping if desired.

Try this:
Follow the traditional presentation of moon cakes by also serving fruits cut into "moon-shaped" pieces. Try melon balls, round slices of oranges or apples, pineapple rings, etc.

Harvest Hare

The hare is a very common symbol associated with the Moon Festival. One legend says that a hare can be seen in the moon. It is told that he sits under a cassia tree where he creates a potion for long life.

Materials:
White paper plates, hare pattern, yellow and gray construction paper, crayons or markers, yarn, star stickers, hole punch, scissors, glue

Preparation:
Use the pattern to make a simple hare shape for each child from the gray paper. Help the children cut out the hares if necessary. Cut a large circle for each child from the yellow paper.

Activity:
Let the children glue the yellow circle to their paper plate. Next have them glue on the hare shape. They may color in eyes and a nose if they wish. Let them add a few bright stars to the background, then punch a hole at the top of the plate and string with yarn to hang.

Extension:
Talk with the children about "the man in the moon." Ask them to look at the moon in the evening and see if they can imagine a rabbit under a tree. Discuss what other odd things they've heard about the moon, for example, that it's made of green cheese or that people fall in love under it.

Hare Pattern

The Korean day of thanksgiving is called Chusongal. Traditionally, a band of musicians roams the festival playing music. The music makers shake long ribbons tied around their heads as they beat their cymbals and drums.

Korean Thanksgiving

Activity:
Let the children create their own music with the children's instruments you have on hand. Tie long ribbons around the children's heads or wrists and encourage them to make these dance as they march about and make music.

Chusongal Feast Treats

Special half moon-shaped rice cakes are a traditional festival treat. Why not make your own half-moon treats out of refrigerator-roll sugar cookies?

Ingredients:
Refrigerator-roll sugar cookie dough, half moon cookie cutter, vanilla frosting, tiny silver decorative candy balls, yellow food coloring

Preparation:
Bake the cookies ahead of time and set out to cool. Tint the frosting lightly with the yellow food coloring to make a pale yellow color and set out in several small bowls.

Activity:
Let the children frost their half-moon treats with a plastic knife. Silver candy balls add shimmer.

Moon in the Sky

Who put the moon in the dark night sky? (sung by group)
_____ put the moon in the dark night sky! (group)
Who me? (sung by child named)
Yes, you! (group)
Uh, uh! (child named)
Then who? (group)
_____ put the moon in the dark night sky? (group)
Who me? (child named)
Yes, you! (group)
Uh, uh! (child named)
Then who? (group)

Continue around the circle until every child's name has been used.

In the Good Old Harvest Time

(sing to the tune of "In the Good Old Summertime")

In the good old harvest time,
In the good old harvest time,
Strolling 'neath the yellow moon
With my baby mine.

The moon is bright, yes, bright's the moon,
And that's a very good sign.
That she's your tootsie-wootsie,
In the good old harvest time.

This Jewish holiday celebrated in September or October is a harvest festival commemorating the 40-year period in which the Jews sought shelter in the desert after their exodus from Egypt. The centerpiece of the holiday is the building of a booth or hut called a sukkah, in which meals are eaten. You can create your own sukkah using a refrigerator box.

Building a Sukkah

Materials:
Refrigerator box, pine branches if available, leafy branches, real or artificial leaves, flowers, grasses, poster paints, brushes, craft knife

Preparation:
Cut a door in the refrigerator box. Make slits all around the box.

Activity:
Help the children throw branches across the top of the box. Then have them poke flowers, leaves, and grasses into the slits to give the sukkah a natural look. They may wish to use the poster paints to decorate the sukkah with fruits and vegetables that represent the harvest. Let a few children at a time crawl inside the sukkah for snack time. You may want to cut a hole in the top of the box for a traditional sukkah that is open to the stars.

Treat:
Traditional foods for this celebration are nuts, citrus fruits, and raisins and other dried fruits.

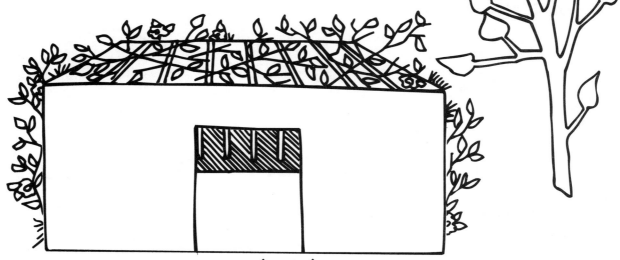

Whether in Canada or the United States, Thanksgiving Day is celebrated with family and friends and includes a feast that usually boasts turkey, corn, squash, and other traditional foods from the countries' earliest successful harvests. Canadian Thanksgiving was once celebrated on the same Thursday as the United States' holiday, but was changed to a Monday for the sake of travelers. In 1931 the holiday was again changed, to October, to be in line with other harvest celebrations.

Patchwork Tablecloth

Materials:
Butcher paper, crayons or markers, scissors, ruler, stapler or tacks (optional)

Preparation:
Measure and cut the butcher paper to the required table size. If desired, cut the paper a bit larger on all sides so it can be stapled or tacked to the table. Use the ruler to mark off patches of equal size.

Activity:
Allow each child to choose a square or two to work on. Large groups might have to work in shifts. Encourage the children to use bright colors and to make any designs they wish. They might experiment with polka dots, stripes, flowers, etc. Put the finished product on the table for a cheerful, homey table covering.

Leafy Collars

Materials:
Extra-large freshly fallen leaves (not dry), extra-long shoelaces

Preparation:
Give a shoelace to each child.

Activity:
Show the children how to carefully poke their shoelace through several leaves and string them together to make a garland to wear around their necks. Make sure each garland is comfortably long so it isn't a danger. Help the children tie off the shoelaces and put on their leafy collars.

Munch a Bunch of Turkey

Ingredients:
Muffins (be sure they're moist so they won't crumble); peeled raw carrots; black olives, drained; toothpicks

Preparation:
Cut the carrots into short, thin spears. Place each muffin on a paper plate. Set out the olives, toothpicks, and carrots.

Activity:
Let all the children create their own little turkey snack. Have them carefully poke three or four carrot spears into the outer edge of the muffin for turkey feathers. For a head, they can place an olive on a toothpick and press it into the muffin's other side. Encourage the children to admire all the creations, give thanks—then remove the toothpick and gobble up!

Stuffed Sweety

Ingredients:
Whole, pitted dates; hazelnuts, walnuts, pecans, almonds, or other large-sized nuts; granulated sugar

Preparation:
Give each child a date or two and place the nuts within reach. Pour granulated sugar over the bottom of a shallow bowl.

Activity:
Let the children stuff their dates by gently pressing a nut into each. Then they may roll the dates in sugar to frost them. The sugar-conscious may skip the frosting step.

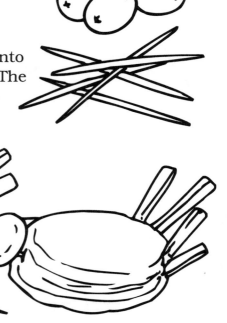

Corn Cob Color Craft

Materials:
Four or five cobs of corn; the same number of large, shallow pans; powdered tempera paints; large sheets of art paper or butcher paper

Preparation:
Mix the paints and pour them evenly in the different pans.

Activity:
Show the children how to roll the cobs of corn in the paint to coat them. Then let them make cob prints on the paper. Encourage the children to experiment with the different colors and with different techniques: rolling the cobs across the paper, pressing the sides of the cobs onto the paper in fan shapes, etc. Let dry completely.

Friendship Branch

Materials:
Dry branches with at least three or four smaller branches shooting out from them, various colors of yarn or thin strips of fabric, scissors, nature items such as long grasses and weeds, feathers, shells, corn husks, seed pods, leaves, etc.

Preparation:
Take the students on a walk to collect the nature items; be sure to point out poisonous plants and to remind the children never to taste anything they pick up. Make sure each child finds an appropriate branch. Cut the fabric or yarn into long lengths.

Activity:
Let the children wind the yarn or fabric strips around the branches any way they like. You might stand ready to help them tie off the ends or tie lengths together. Then encourage the children to decorate their branches with all the items they have collected, tucking them in among the lengths of yarn and fabric.

Extension:
The Indians extended their hands in friendship when they helped the Pilgrims learn how to plant and cultivate the land and survive. Encourage the children to extend their branch of friendship to someone who has helped them. Or they might like to offer it as a Thanksgiving decoration to their family or friends.

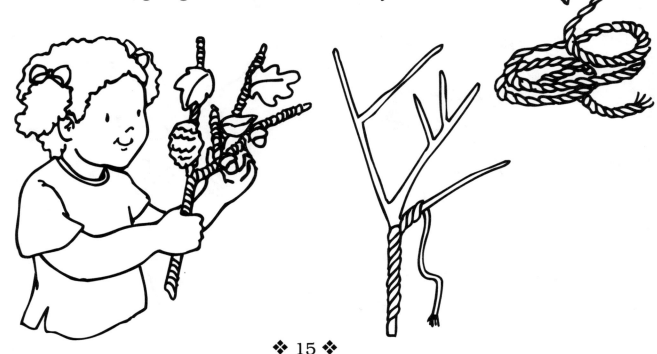

Turkey! Gobble, gobble!

This simple game is a variation of Marco Polo, and always fun.

Materials:
Large, open space for playing, blindfold (optional)

Preparation:
Mark off the playing area with chalk or other markers that delineate the boundaries. Make sure that all the children stay within the boundaries during the game.

Game:
One child is "It" and wears a blindfold or keeps eyes shut tight at all times. All the other children move around within the boundaries and try to avoid being tagged by "It." The child who is "It" keeps calling "Turkey!" and all the other children must answer "Gobble, gobble!" When one of the gobblers is finally located and tagged by "It," that player becomes the next "It."

Squirrels and Nuts

Materials:
Squirrel pattern; toilet paper tubes; snack cups small enough to fit inside toilet tube sections; a variety of nuts, raisins, and jellied fruit snacks; crayons; scissors; glue or stapler

Preparation:
Make a copy of the pattern for each child and cut the patterns out if necessary. Cut the tubes into small sections. Fill the snack cups with treats and hide one for each child about the room.

Activity:
Begin by having the children color their squirrel patterns. Then help them to staple or glue the bottom edge to the tube section. Have the children stand their squirrels up at their desk or in a play area. Then they can pretend to be little squirrels gathering nuts for the winter. Invite them to move about the room and hunt for a snack cup full of goodies. As soon as they find one, they should return to their squirrel and place the cup in the tube section. For those having trouble locating a cup, use the standard "hot" and "cold" clues.

Squirrel Pattern

Turkey Trot Action Verse

I'm a turkey, watch me trot.
A chicken I am not!
(Point to self, then flap arms and trot in place.)

I'm a turkey, hear me gobble.
When I walk, see me wobble!
(Point to self, flap arms, and wobble back and forth.)

I'm a turkey, growing wide.
When Thanksgiving comes—I'll hide!
(Hold arms out to side, then cover face and fall to ground.)

Corn o' Plenty Action Verse

Cobs of corn,
Munch! Munch! Munch!
(Pretend to munch corn on the cob.)

Popping corn,
Pop! Pop! Pop!
(Hop up and down.)

Cornmeal mush,
Mash! Mash! Mash!
(Grind one palm into the other.)

Corn bread stuffing,
Yum! Yum! Yum!
(Rub tummy up and down.)

Gobble, gobble!

The Animals' Thanksgiving Action Verse

Seeds for the birds
And the birds give thanks.
Tweet! Tweet! Tweet!
(Flap arms and tweet sweetly.)

Carrots for the bunnies,
And the bunnies give thanks.
Hop! Hop! Hop!
(Put hands up like paws and hop.)

Bugs for the chicks,
And the chicks give thanks.
Cheep! Cheep! Cheep!
(Nod head up and down and cheep.)

Succotash Mash Action Verse

Lima beans and corn are the typical succotash ingredients. Here the children act out the making of this traditional Thanksgiving dish.

Pick the beans
And shuck the corn.
(Make picking and shucking motions.)

Mix 'em all up,
And cook 'em in the 'morn.
(Pretend to stir in a pot.)

Do the succotash mash!
(Clap, clap.)
Succotash!

Do the succotash mash!
(Clap, clap.)
Succotash!

(Repeat.)

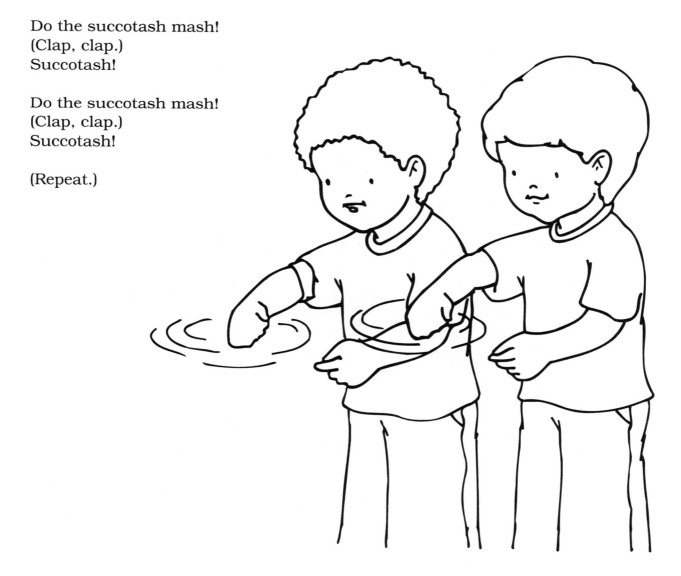

It's Thanksgiving!

(sing to the tune of "London Bridge Is Falling Down")

See the Pilgrims sailing in, sailing in, sailing in.
See the Pilgrims sailing in, it's Thanksgiving!

See them landing on that rock, on that rock, on that rock.
See them landing on that rock, it's Thanksgiving!

Watch them toil and work the land, work the land, work the land.
Watch them toil and work the land, it's Thanksgiving!

Indians will help them plant, help them plant, help them plant.
Indians will help them plant, it's Thanksgiving!

Now they'll gather for a feast, for a feast, for a feast.
Now they'll gather for a feast, it's Thanksgiving!

We might think of July and August as the harvest time for the northwest coast Koyukon Indian people, since this is the time most salmon are caught. The Koyukon traditionally dried whatever salmon was not eaten fresh to make this resource last all year long. Salmon are still important to the Koyukon people and thought of as very powerful. Children wear dried salmon tails around their necks or carry them in their pockets to keep them from harm.

Salmon Tail Necklace

Materials:
Salmon tail pattern, markers, hole punch, construction paper, scissors, glue, yarn

Preparation:
Make a copy of the pattern for each child and cut them out. Also cut out a tail-size piece of construction paper for each child.

Activity:
Let the children use markers to color the tails with vibrant colors. Then let them glue the salmon tails to the construction paper. Let the children make a hole in the end of their tail, string with yarn, and wear around their neck for good luck.

Salmon Tail Pattern

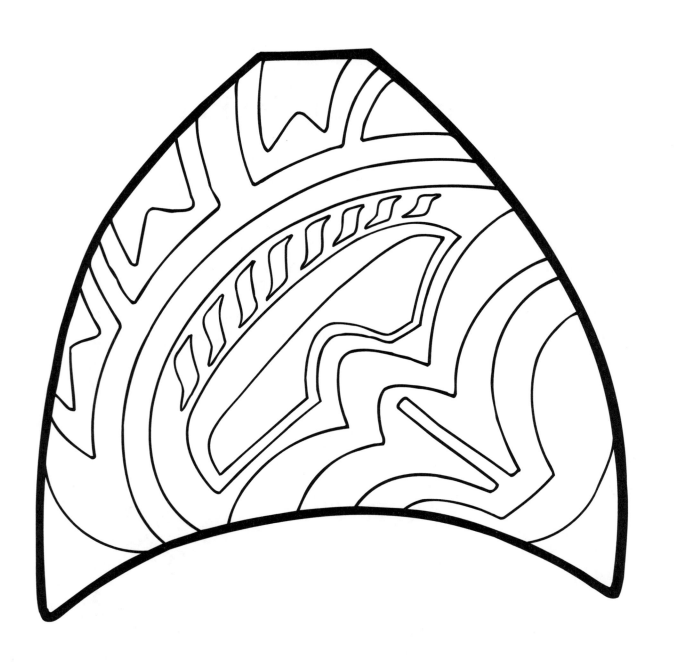

Ashura is a holiday of thanksgiving celebrated by Moslems. It commemorates the occasion of Noah, his family, and his ark full of animals surviving the flood. Tradition says that Noah's wife prepared a special pudding called ashura the first day Noah was able to set foot on land.

Noah's Ark

Materials:
Cardboard box, foam egg carton, construction paper, scissors, glue, hay or straw, craft knife, small plastic or stuffed animals

Preparation:
Remove the top from the box and place the open box on the floor. Let the children cut window and door shapes from the paper and glue them on to decorate the "ark." To make steps coming from the boat to the ground, make a slit in the box with the craft knife and poke the sectioned half of the egg carton into the cardboard.

Activity:
Place straw or hay in the bottom of the box and encourage the children to bring small plastic or stuffed animals from home to complete the ark scene.

Ashura Pudding

Ingredients:
Prepared vanilla pudding; traditional ashura ingredients including dates, figs, grapes, and nuts

Preparation:
Cut or chop the grapes and other fruits and nuts into small pieces. Let the children help you stir them into the pudding in a large mixing bowl.

Treat:
Put spoonfuls of the pudding into aluminum baking cups for individual servings.

Try this:
For a group of finicky eaters, offer the treat as a "pudding bar." Set out the fruits and nuts in individual bowls and let the children top their puddings with the additions of their choice.

English Christmas Pieces

In England the first Christmas cards were created when schoolboys made "Christmas pieces" to show off their best writing efforts.

Materials:
Green or yellow construction paper, white paper doilies, crayons, scissors, paste

Preparation:
Cut large Christmas tree or bell shapes from the green or yellow paper, one for each child.

Activity:
Let each child paste a doily to the center of a tree or bell. Then have the children write their name on the center of the doily or draw a special picture. Encourage them to give this "Christmas piece" to a favorite someone.

Klasses

In Belgium, St. Nicholas brings children toys, gifts, and klasses—sweet flat cakes like these with the children's initials on them.

Ingredients:
Flat sugar cookies or graham crackers, colored frosting in squeeze tubes (if necessary, add attachments that produce a thin line)

Preparation:
Set out the different tubes of frosting and give each child a cookie or cracker.

Treats:
Let the children experiment with the frosting and decorate their cookies or crackers. Have them save room in the middle to write their initials.

Holiday Traditions

In Norway, roast pig is the traditional feast item for Christmas celebrations. Another tradition is to pass out bowls of sweetened porridge sprinkled with cinnamon and sugar; an almond is hidden in one of the bowls. The person who finds the almond usually hides it beneath his or her tongue until everyone finishes, then announces the discovery. The lucky winner is given a small marzipan pig.

Try this:
Your children can experience the Norwegian tradition with hot or cold cereal. For a very young group, hide a raisin instead of a hard almond. Give the winner an inexpensive plastic toy pig instead of candy.

Combine serving the treat with making simple pig faces on paper plates. Have the children paste on their paper plate a circle cut from gray construction paper. Let them glue on a pink round nose and eyes. Then have them glue googly eyes to the centers of the eyes and add pink ears.

Heart Baskets

Activity:
At Christmas time, Norwegians enjoy creating baskets from paper hearts. Let the children staple the edges of two paper hearts together, leaving the top open, add a paper handle, fill with candies, and hang on a Christmas tree.

Stocking Surprises

In the United States we hang stockings on the fireplace at Christmas. The story behind this tradition is that the real St. Nick wished to help the very poor father of three girls who had no money for a dowry. He tossed gold down the family's chimney and it landed in a stocking that was hung by the fire to dry.

Activity:

At rest time have the children remove one sock and set it in a special place, out of sight. While they sleep, place a tangerine into the toe of each sock to represent a lump of gold.

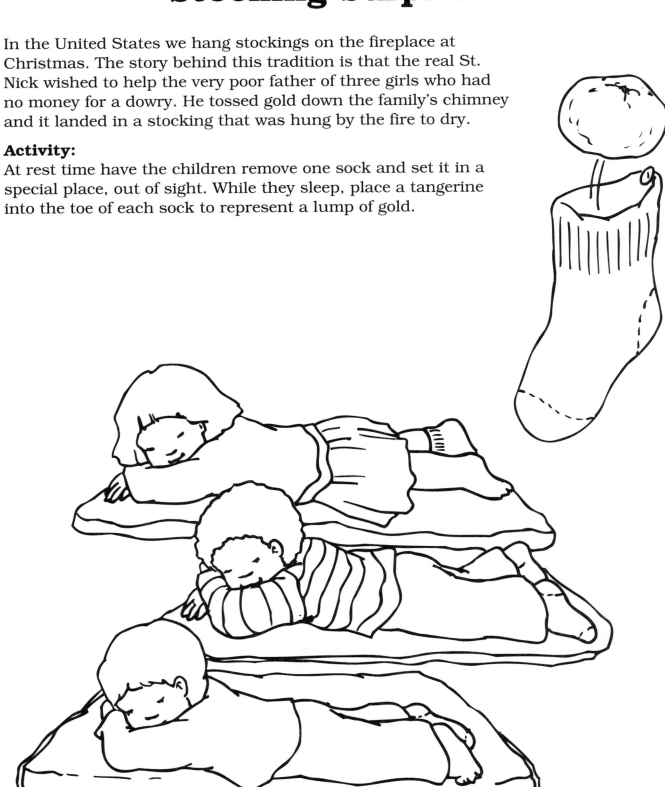

Shoe Surprises

Children in Italy and France set their shoes out the night before Christmas. If they've been good they find them filled with treats in the morning. Why not have your children set their shoes out of sight during naptime and later find them filled with little treats? Or let them make shoes for you to fill with wrapped goodies.

Materials:
Construction paper, sequins, buttons, glitter, ribbon, hole punch and yarn (optional), markers, glue, scissors

Preparation:
Trace the children's feet (shoes on) and then cut out the shapes. Punch holes for shoelaces if the children want to lace the shoes with yarn.

Activity:
If you've made lace holes, let the children string the yarn through. Otherwise, the children may decorate the shoes with sequins, buttons, glitter, or bows. Be sure each child's shoes are labeled before they're set out at rest time.

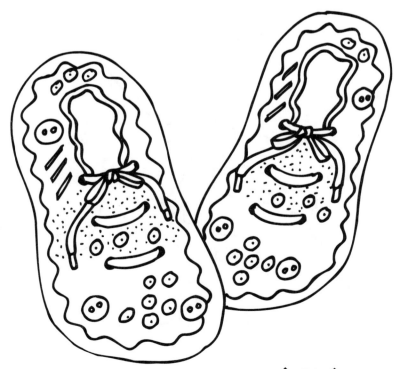

Gumdrop Starburst

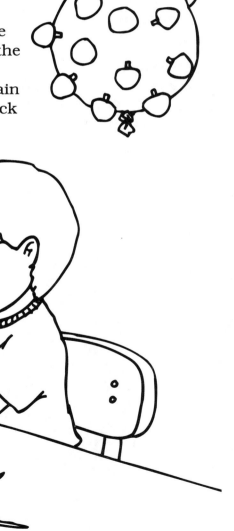

Children can help make this craft and then unmake it later.

Materials:
Styrofoam ball (or an apple or orange), toothpicks, small colored gumdrops, large needle or bodkin, ribbon, knife (optional)

Preparation:
For each starburst, knot one end of a length of ribbon and thread it through the needle. Pull the ribbon through the Styrofoam ball or piece of fruit from bottom to top. (You may need to start the insertion hole with a knife.) Remove the needle and loop and tie the ribbon end for hanging.

Activity:
Let the children sit at a table and push one gumdrop onto the end of each toothpick. When they are done, have them poke the other end of all the toothpicks into the ball for a gumdrop starburst. Hang the starbursts around the room and, at certain times, let the children pull off a gumdrop, leaving the toothpick behind.

Glittering Garland

Materials:
Straws, jumbo round sequins with holes, yarn, tape, scissors

Preparation:
Cut the straws into short sections. Put tape around an end of a yarn length for each child to use as a threader.

Activity:
Let the children make garlands by threading straws and sequins alternately on the yarn. Tie the ends. You may also want to have them string macaroni dyed with food coloring and thread spools decorated with glitter or paper. Or let the children make edible garlands of pretzels, Cheerios, or dried apple or pineapple rings.

Santa Says

Activity:
Play a variation of Simon Says using Santa. Santa can give commands such as wrap a gift, ring a bell, put on boots, throw a snowball, eat a Christmas cookie, and say Noel, and the children can mimic the actions.

Stocking Stitch-Up

Materials:
Construction paper, hole punch, scissors, yarn, tape, glue, a variety of decorative materials such as glitter, sticker stars, markers, etc.

Preparation:
Create a simple stocking pattern and cut two shapes for each child from the construction paper. Place the two patterns together and punch holes, spaced at intervals, all along the sides and bottom. Cut yarn lengths and tape one end tightly to thread easily.

Activity:
Have the children stitch up their stockings, then help them tie off the yarn ends. They may decorate their stockings in any way they wish. The finished stockings are a great way to send home drawings—just roll them up and tuck inside!

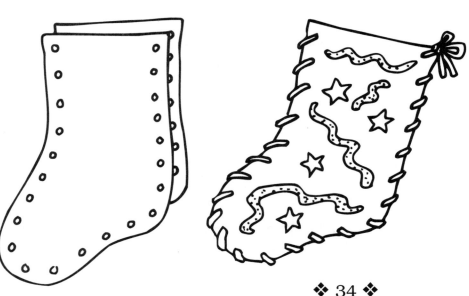

Muffin Tin Toss

Materials:

Six-, nine-, or twelve-hole muffin tin; circles of white paper; holiday stickers or colored markers; small prizes such as pencil-top erasers, plastic combs or pins, boxes of raisins, individually wrapped hard candies, stickers, new loose crayons, fancy pencils, etc.; paper lunch bags; pennies

Preparation:

With the stickers or markers, mark each of 6, 9, or 12 paper circles (depending on muffin tin size) with a different Christmas symbol (star, snowflake, tree, bell, etc.). Put a paper circle in the bottom of each tin hole. Place corresponding marks on lunch bags. Distribute the prizes among the lunch bags.

Activity:

Give each child a penny. One at a time have the children stand a few feet away from the muffin tin and toss the penny in it. They should match the hole the penny lands in with the marked bag, and reach in for a prize. The game can also match colors, shapes, letters, or small words. Continue the game until every child has received a prize.

It Ain't Gonna Snow No More

(sing to the tune of "It Ain't Gonna Rain No More")

It ain't gonna snow, no more, no more.
It ain't gonna snow no more.
How in the world can I _____
If it ain't gonna snow no more?!

Have the children sit in a circle and takes turns filling in the
blank with something they might not be able to do without
snow. Examples are sled on the hill, skate on the pond, ski
down the mountain, throw a snowball, build a snowman. Don't
worry about the rhythm as the children contribute to the song.

Santa Had a Little Friend

(sing to the tune of "Mary Had a Little Lamb")

Santa had a little friend,
Little friend, little friend.
Santa had a little friend,
Its nose was red as (pause) snow?
No! (Shout it out.)

And everywhere that Santa went,
Santa went, Santa went,
Everywhere that Santa went
That friend was sure to go!

His nose, it shined so red and bright,
Red and bright, red and bright.
His nose, it shined so red and bright
On Santa's sleigh that night.

He led the way through snow and hail,
Snow and hail, snow and hail.
He led the way through snow and hail,
So Santa wouldn't fail.

Rudolph was his name, you know,
His nose did glow, his nose did glow.
Rudolph was his name, you know,
His nose was red as (pause) snow?
No! (Shout it out.)

In the period from early to late spring, many countries throughout the world celebrate one of these pre-Lent festivities. They're generally boisterous events lasting at least three days, filled with merry-making, fun, and frolicking in the streets. The celebrations are marked by feasting, parades, colorful decorations including a profusion of flowers, costumes and masks, and games. In this section you'll find several ideas for games, crafts, and activities that highlight customs from around the world.

Costumed Characters

Materials:

Long scarves or glittery strips of fabric; old hats of any sort; colorful vests and blouses; silly ties, boas, wraps, or faux fur stoles; dangly, jangly costume jewelry including clip earrings, necklaces, and bracelets; non-toxic face paints; tissues; hand mirrors and, if available, a full-length mirror

Preparation:

Children can help collect the costume pieces. Send a note home a few days before your celebration so that parents can search for suitable contributions from the far reaches of their closets. Set out all the costume pieces so that the children can view the possibilities. Place the face paint and the hand mirrors on a low table so that they can experiment.

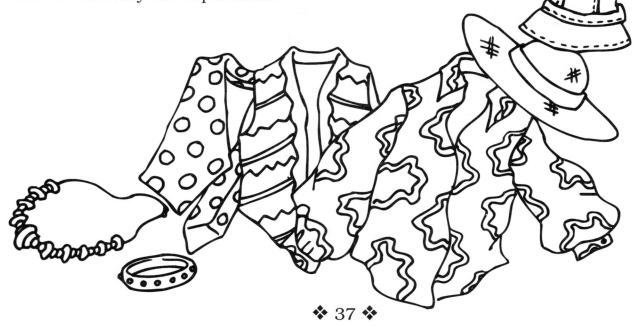

Activity:

Allow the children to spend time trying on costumes. Encourage them to try several before deciding. Then let them paint their faces as they like. Or they may choose to wear a mask (directions and patterns for making masks follow).

When your costumed revelers are ready, choose a parade route and put on a show! Let the children walk around the block, down the hall past the next class, or simply entertain themselves with a jaunt through the play area. You might allow the children to carry tambourines or other noisemakers, or simply carry a small cassette player and turn on some festive music as you lead the parade!

If you have spectators, and you wish to do so, it is traditional in Carnaval parades to throw flowers and treats to the crowd. Try having the children hand out peanuts in the shell, mini boxes of raisins, pennies, small wrapped candies, and real or plastic flowers.

Latin American Carnaval parades feature beautiful, sometimes intricate costumes with beads, feathers, and sequins. The following masks will add color to the children's parade, but will also be comfortable and safe because they're worn across the forehead and bridge of the nose, leaving the eyes uncovered.

Masked Merriment

Materials:
Fluorescent colors of lightweight poster board, mask pattern, colored craft feathers, flat sequins (all sizes), elastic, scissors, pen, markers, hole punch, brushes, thick craft glue, stapler

Preparation:
Use the pattern to create a mask for each child. Punch holes where noted. Bend each mask slightly, right in the middle, so it will hug the face. Use one child as a model and decide on the proper length of elastic to hold on the mask. Loop one end through a hole and staple. Staple the other side. Now cut the elastic for the other masks. Set aside. Set out the decorative materials.

Activity:
Allow the children to create any type of fantastical mask they choose. Encourage them to paste on sequins, outline the eyes with markers, or add feathers across the top. Let their imaginations run wild! When the masks are completed, be sure to have them dry thoroughly.

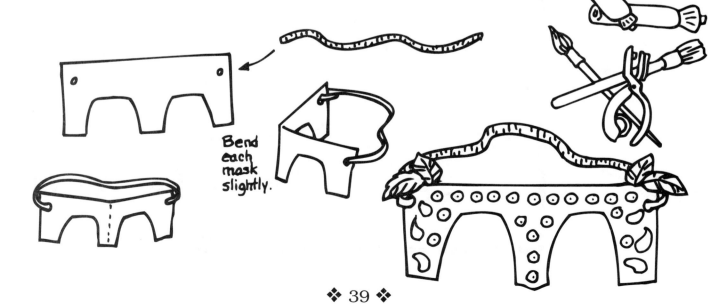

Bend each mask slightly.

Mask Pattern

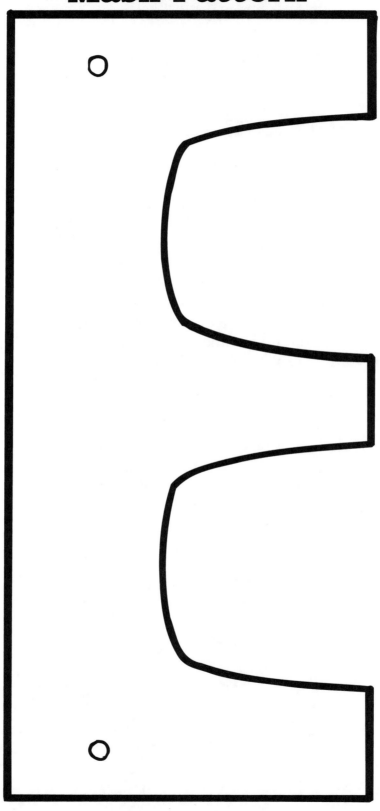

Streamer Surprise

In Spain, showers of confetti and streamers are a big part of any Mardi Gras parade or party. Don't forget yours!

Materials:
Paper party serpentines, toilet paper tubes, crayons or markers, stickers, glitter, glue, brushes, scissors, wide masking or postal tape, regular masking tape

Preparation:
Cover one end of a tube for each child with a piece of wide masking or postal tape. Set out all the decorating materials. Tear off a small piece of regular masking tape for each child (about half a finger's length) and place the pieces on the edge of a table so they can be reached easily. Carefully separate the serpentine rolls.

Activity:
Let the children decorate their tubes in any way they wish, pressing on stickers, coloring, or gluing on glitter. Let the tubes dry completely.

One at a time, gently pull free the loose end on the inside of a serpentine and, using the small pieces of tape, stick it to the inside of the open end of one of the children's tubes. Drop the remaining coil inside the tube. Then demonstrate throwing the serpentine: without letting go of the tube, simply give a quick forward flick. Remind the children to hold their tubes upright until they're ready to use them. Let them carry their Streamer Surprises during a parade and send them streaming when the spirit moves them!

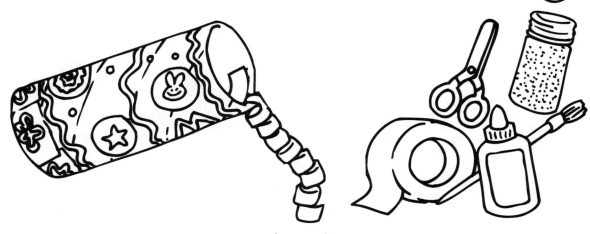

Fantasy Fairy Tale Floats

In the Virgin Islands a parade is held especially for children, with all the floats featuring fairy tale characters. Encourage the children to create their own floats using fairy tale or nursery rhyme themes. The following are ideas for parade or display floats based on Humpty Dumpty, the King and Queen of Hearts, Cinderella, and Jack in the Beanstalk.

Materials:
Shoe boxes (covered with paper if desired); character patterns; medium-size plastic eggs (the kind you fill); king and queen of hearts playing cards; old magazines; Easter grass or shredded green tissue paper; pastel-colored tissue paper; real, plastic, or straw flowers; crepe paper streamers; glitter or confetti; googly eyes (optional); lightweight cardboard; crayons; scissors; glue; stapler; permanent black marker; tape; knife

Preparation:
Lay out all the materials and any others you might think of for flamboyant shoe box floats. Twist together strips of pastel-colored tissue paper and tape the ends to create fluffy flowers. Make copies of the patterns and cut out pieces of cardboard roughly the shape of the patterns for backing.

Activity:
For the floats, start by having the children overturn their shoe box, spread it with glue, and press on Easter grass or shredded tissue. Let them glue on a profusion of straw, plastic, or tissue flowers; pictures cut from magazines; and a sprinkling of glitter or confetti. They can even add crepe paper streamers to one end. To make Cinderella and Jack from Jack and the Beanstalk, let the children color in the patterns and cut them out; help with the cutting if necessary. Then glue the patterns to the cardboard backings. For the other characters, and for ideas on placing the characters on the floats, see the following.

Fantasy Fairy Tale Floats

Cinderella:
Make a slit in the float and help the children slip in the completed pattern. If available, glue on a doll shoe for a perfect touch.

Humpty Dumpty:
The children can use the marker to draw a frowning face on the top half of the plastic egg. Then they can glue on two googly eyes, or draw them in. Have them glue Humpty Dumpty's two halves separately to the float. If desired, make a slit in the float and help the children slip in a piece of cardboard for the wall.

Jack and the Beanstalk:
Make a slit in the float and help the children slip in the completed pattern. Glue on a bean or two if you have any.

King and Queen:
Make a short slit in the float and help the children slip in a corner of the king and queen of hearts playing cards.

Try this:
Let the children parade around the room holding their floats, or set the floats up as a display. Afterward, read some picture books to the children about characters from their floats. Or check out and show one of the many Fairy Tale Theater videos from your local library or video store.

❖•❖•❖•❖•❖•❖•❖•❖•❖•❖•❖•❖•❖•❖•❖•❖

Jack and the Beanstalk Pattern

Cinderella Pattern

Carnaval Commotion Action Verse

Carnaval colors!
(Make raining motions with fingers.)
Carnaval delight!
(Frame face with thumbs on chin, and grin.)
Carnaval commotion!
(Shake arms and wiggle hips.)
In a mask tonight!
(Hold fingers over eyes like mask.)

Repeat.

Get the Carnaval Beat!

Collect a simple musical instrument or noisemaker for each child, such as harmonicas, baby rattles, and small party horns (or have the children make "Shaker Makers"). Have the children perform the following action verse, holding their instruments at their sides until the last line, keeping their dominant hand free for gesturing.

Carnaval means yummy treats!
(Rub tummy with free hand.)
Carnaval means cakes so sweet!
(Bring fingers to lips and kiss.)
Carnaval means marching feet!
(Stomp up and down.)
Drums that beat!
(Slap side with free hand.)
And music in the street!
(Lift instrument and blow or shake away!)

Shaker Makers

Materials:

Empty, small plastic containers (prescription bottles, spice jars) with tight-fitting lids; an assortment of grains and beans in different sizes, such as rice, popcorn kernels, pinto or small red beans, or split peas; muffin tin

Preparation:

Wash and dry the bottles, removing all labels, and distribute to the children. Set each type of bean and grain in a different section of the muffin tin.

Activity:

Allow the children to place a small amount of the materials in their containers, put on the top, and then shake. Encourage them to experiment with the different beans and listen for the different sounds. If the children are using prescription bottles with safety caps, you may have to stand nearby and help them take the caps on and off. When they have decided on the sound they like best, help them put the bottle cap on tight. Let them use their Shaker Makers with the "Get the Carnaval Beat!" action verse.

Flowers, Flowers, Falling Down

(sing to the tune of "London Bridge Is Falling Down")

Give each child a paper bag full of real, straw, plastic, or tissue paper flowers to use at the end of this song. You can easily make tissue paper flowers by twisting together small colored pieces of the paper and taping the ends.

Flowers, flowers, falling down,
Falling down, falling down.
(Hold hands, go around in a circle.)
Flowers, flowers, falling down,
(Hold hands up, walk into center.)
Go parading!

Take the flowers, throw them 'round,
Throw them 'round, throw them 'round.
(Hold hands, go around in circle again.)
Take the flowers, throw them 'round,
(Hold hands up, walk into center.)
Go parading!
(Shake out bag of flowers.)

A Carnaval of Colors

(sing to the tune of "Ring Around the Rosies")

As the children sing and play this fun circle game, let them toss confetti or their Streamer Surprises for additional colorful fun! If they use their Streamer Surprises, demonstrate how to throw them by holding the edge of the tube while you give a quick forward flick.

March around the village (or city),
A pocketful of color!
Flashes! Flashes!
We all call . . . STOP!
(Stretch out the last line, pausing with suspense
    before yelling "STOP!" and giving a stomp.)

March around the village (or city),
A pocketful of color!
Flashes! Flashes!
We all call . . . STOP!
(Stretch out the last line, pausing with suspense
    before yelling "STOP!" and giving a stomp.)

March around the village (or city),
A pocketful of color!
Flashes! Flashes!
We all call . . . CARNAVAL!
(Again, pause for suspense, then yell
    "CARNAVAL!" and toss the
confetti or
    flick the Streamer Surprise.)

On a Carnaval Spree

Let the children sing and dance with this action verse.

Dancing, dancing, wild and free!
(Wiggle and spin.)
Under a cape, who could I be?
(Fold arm across face like a villain.)
Behind a mask, what do I see?
(Hold hands up to face like a mask.)
I could be you!
(Point to another child.)
I could be me!
(Point to self.)
Dancing, dancing, wild and free!
(Wiggle and spin.)

Queen Esther was a beautiful Jewish woman who was chosen to be the queen of King Ahasuerus of Persia. Haman was the king's prime minister, who somehow convinced Ahasuerus to kill all the Jews. Through cunning and bravery, Queen Esther convinced the king to allow the Jews to arm themselves. They did, and defeated the evil Haman. Ever since, Purim has been a joyous holiday that celebrate's this event. Children dress up as Queen Esther, King Ahasuerus, and the evil Haman. They hold carnivals, parties, and parades with noisemakers.

Royal Masquerade

Materials:
10-inch stiff white paper plates (microwave-safe paper plates work well), 7-inch round bowl or plate, craft knife, cutting surface, stickers, confetti, colorful construction paper, glue

Preparation:
Cut a 7-inch hole from the center of a paper plate; you can trace around the bowl or plate and then cut with a craft knife. Place the paper plate like a crown on one of your student's heads to see if it fits; adjust if necessary. Make one for each child.

Activity:
Have the children decorate the underside of their plate rim with confetti, paper pieces, stickers, and the like.

Try this:
Bring in royal garments for the children to wear with their crowns: colorful capes, vests, scarves, beads and jewelry, sashes, and large buckled belts. Then have a party or a parade.

Hamantash

Traditional foods for Purim include hamantash, or Haman's Ear, a sweet three-cornered pastry-like cake filled with honey. Try this simple version.

Ingredients:
White sandwich bread (or poppyseed loaf cake for a more traditional version), honey

Preparation:
Cut the crusts from the bread slices, or slice the loaf cake.

Activity:
Let the children use plastic knives to help spread honey on the sandwich slices or cake pieces, then have each place two pieces together. Cut into triangles.

Many stories are attributed to St. Patrick of Ireland, including one that credits him with leading all the snakes out of the country. Today, St. Patrick's Day is celebrated anywhere that people wish to pay tribute to or celebrate their Irish heritage. The wearing of something green is, of course, the preferred costume of the day, and the pinch is the trick if you're found not sporting some sort of green attire! Wearing green may be a custom that developed from the yearly burning of green boughs and leaves each spring in order to make the soil richer.

St. Paddy's Match-up

Materials:
St. Patrick's Day patterns, green construction paper, crayons, scissors, glue, envelopes

Preparation:
Make two copies of each pattern for each child. Also cut out a green paper rectangle for each pattern to be glued to after coloring.

Activity:
Let each child color in all the patterns and then cut them out. Have them glue each picture to a paper rectangle to provide a stiff backing. After playing the game in school, encourage the children to take their pattern pieces home in an envelope and share the matching game with family members.

Game:
Turn all the pattern pieces face down on a table. Playing in pairs, let the children take turns flipping over two pieces in order to find a match. If no match is found, the child should turn the pieces face down again. If a match is found, the player earns a second turn. Play continues until all matches have been found. To make the game last longer, include another set of pattern pieces.

Patterns

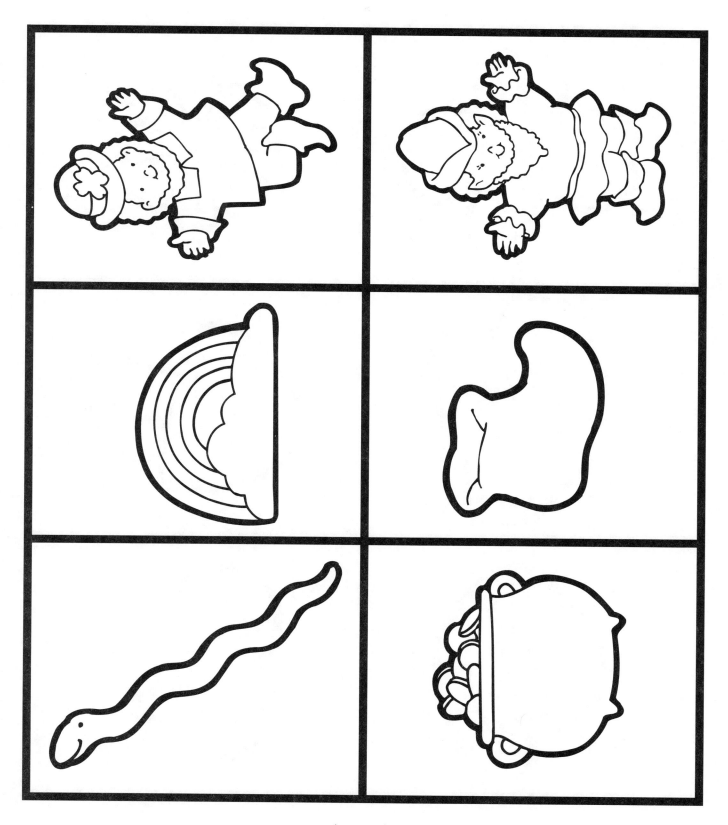

Patterns

Bagels and Green Cheese

Many St. Patrick's Day celebrations include partaking of green-colored foods and drinks. Offer the class this green version of a popular snack.

Ingredients:
Sliced plain bagels, cream cheese, green food coloring

Preparation:
Add a small amount of food coloring to the cream cheese and mix well. Start with just a tiny bit—it doesn't take much!

Treat:
Allow the children to use plastic knives to spread the green cheese on their own bagels. Eat up!

Shamrock Soda

Ingredients:
Sparkling water or lemon-lime soda (tint green with food coloring), thin slices of lime, green ice cubes (tint fresh water with food coloring), clear plastic cups, bendable straws

Treat:
Pour a cupful of water or soda for each child. Let the children plop in an ice cube and a slice of lime.

More Green Goodies to Gobble:
Mint jelly spread on water crackers; a green fruit salad made with green grapes, kiwis, green apples, and honeydew melon; lime jello; mint ice cream topped with green-tinted whipped cream.

Color 'n Crunch

This is a quick St. Patrick's-theme activity that also reinforces shapes and colors—and it tastes good too!

Materials:
Lucky Charms cereal, small bowls

Preparation:
Pour each child some Lucky Charms cereal.

Activity:
Let the children work on picking out all the marshmallows. Then have them sort the pieces by shape. Let the children munch on a bit of the cereal while working. After the shapes are sorted, have the children identify the colors and then ask them to name other things that are the same colors.

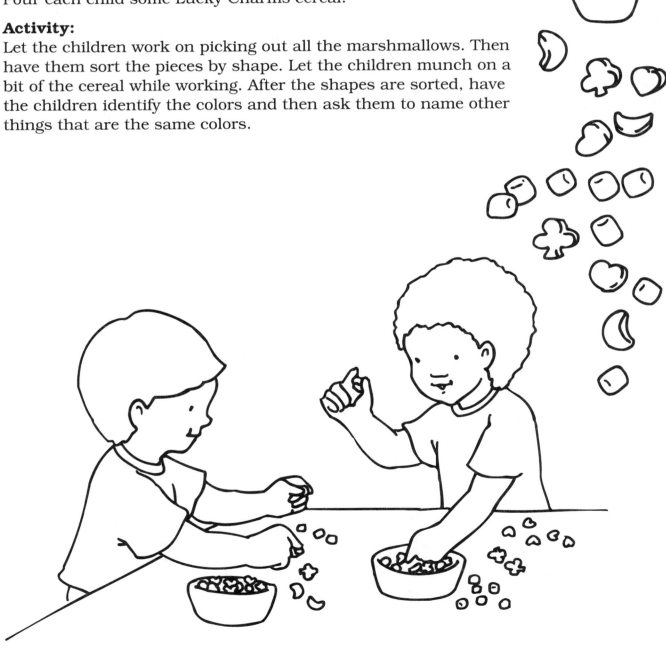

Snakes Alive

Materials:
Bright green felt, green metallic pipe cleaners, silver or gold glitter, scissors, glue

Preparation:
For each snake, cut two tapered strips of felt just a little shorter than the length of the pipe cleaners.

Activity:
Have the children spread liberal amounts of glue on the felt pieces. Then they can place a pipe cleaner in the middle of one piece of felt so that the end of the pipe cleaner hangs off the narrow end of the felt. Have the children place the other piece of felt on top, and press together to secure. Let dry. Then encourage the children to glue on spots of glitter for eyes. Show the children how to bend the snake gently and curl the end of the metallic pipe cleaner.

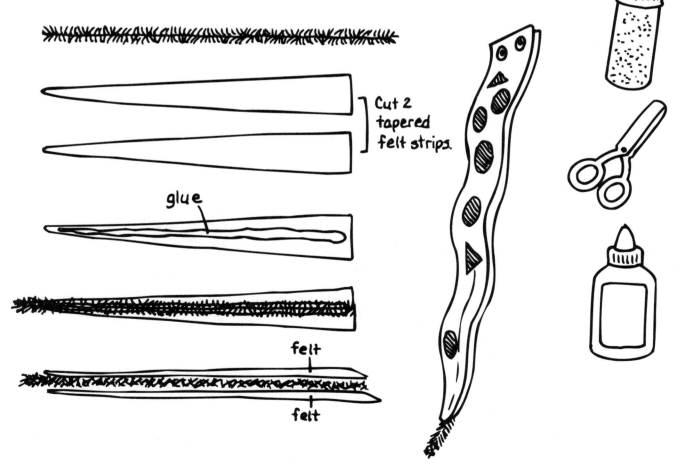

Cut 2 tapered felt strips.

glue

felt

felt

Irish Potato Stew Action Verse

The children will enjoy acting out the making of a delicious Irish stew.

One potato, two potato, three potato, four.
(Hold up one, two, three, then four fingers, keeping them up.)
Stir 'em up, stir 'em up, we want more!
(Curl arm like bowl, stir with other hand.)
Five potato, six potato, seven potato, more!
(Hold up five, six, seven fingers, then all ten.)
Stir 'em up, stir 'em up, we want more!
(Pretend to stir a big cooking pot.)

Cut up the carrots, cut up the meat,
(Make cutting motions.)
Put 'em in the pot, and turn up the heat!
(Make tossing motion, then flick wrist as though turning dial.)
Knife and fork, and napkin too.
(Hold left hand out, then right, then pretend to tie napkin at
    neck.)
Now I'm ready for Irish stew!
(Rub tummy.)

Corned Beef and Cabbage

These two action verses will bring out the ham (or corned beef!) in the children.

Corned beef and cabbage
Stewing in the pot!
(Stir a big pot.)
Big round potatoes,
Cookin' up hot!
(Rub tummy and lick lips.)
Cook and cook, simmer and stew!
(Stir pot, shimmy shoulders, squat down.)
Then it's dinner for me and you!
(Pop up, point to self, then audience.)

Slap, Slap Shenanigans!

Slap, slap shenanigans,
(Slap knees twice, then clap.)
Do an Irish jig!
(Put hands on hips, and kick out.)
Hello, lass!
(Boys tip their hats.)
Hello, laddie!
(Girls curtsy.)
Slap, slap shenanigans,
(Slap knees twice, then clap.)
Do an Irish jig!
(Put hands on hips, and kick out.)

Poisson d'Avril, or April fish, is what French people call the person who has been tricked on April First. April Fool's Day dates back to 16th-century France, but no one is really sure of its origin. Some say it may have to do with the change of seasons—spring seems to trick us by quickly changing from sun to showers. Or it may have to do with the zodiac sign Pisces, the fish. People sent fake presents to one another or sent each other on impossible errands. Today, bakeries decorate with chocolate fish, and people send fish-decorated postcards to one another.

Chocolate Fish

Combine the very traditional April Fool's Day fish with a chocolate treat!

Materials:
Chocolate kisses, fish pattern, paper towel or toilet paper tubes, different colors of construction paper, masking tape, Scotch tape, scissors, glue, glitter, markers, thin ribbon streamers, googly eyes (optional)

Preparation:
Cut the tubes into small sections. Trace and cut two fish pattern pieces for each child from colored paper. Close one end of the tube sections with masking tape. Set out glue, Scotch tape, and decorative materials.

Activity:
Show the children how to wrap one fish pattern over a tube and tape down. (The tail extends out past the closed end. About an inch of paper extends beyond the other side of the tube.) Now they can tape on the second fish, matching up the tail sections. If desired, let them glue the tail sections together with some ribbons streaming out. Or they may glue on two googly eyes, color in scales with markers, and glue on glitter. When the fish are dry, fill with the chocolate treats, and push the ends of the paper down in to close.

Fish Pattern

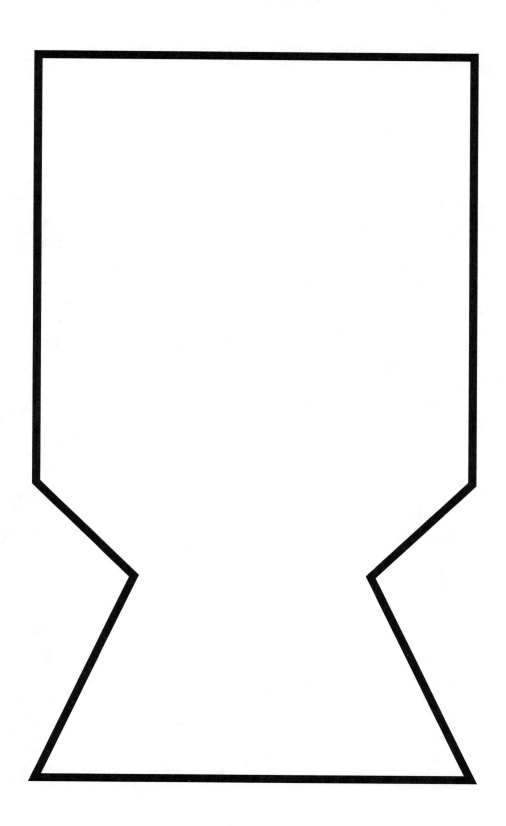

April Fool's Fishy Prints

The children may use these cards to send a traditional April Fool's greeting.

Materials:
Stamped postcards, ink pads, colored paper, green and blue glitter and glue mixture, brushes, glue, scissors, black fine-point markers

Preparation:
Cut tiny triangles (a little smaller than your thumb) from many colors of paper. Set out the ink pads.

Activity:
First, encourage the children to paint a shiny sea border around their cards with the glitter mixture. Next, they can glue on about three or four triangles for fish tails; they should leave plenty of room in between. Show the children how to press their thumbs onto the ink pad and make a thumb print on the pointy end of the triangles for a personalized fish. (Have paper towels available for smudged thumbs.) Later, they can add an eye with the marker. Tell the children they can send this "April Fish" card to an unsuspecting friend.

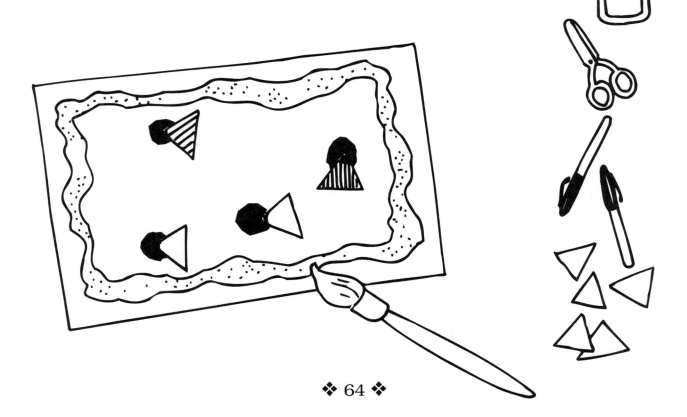

April Fool's Tricky Chicks

Play this game for a spot of fun on a spring day.

Materials:
A defined play area

Preparation:
Explain the game to the children. Choose someone to be the hen and mark a corner of the room for the hen's roosting spot.

Activity:
Send your hen out of the room. Choose about three or four chicks from your group. All the children, including the chicks, should cup two hands over their mouths, and keep them covered, to trick the hen. When the hen returns, she calls, "Cluck, cluck, cluck," trying to find the chicks. Everyone should answer, but only the three chicks should actually say, "Peep, peep, peep." Have the hen walk around calling, "Cluck, cluck, cluck" until a chick is identified. The chick then goes off to wait in the roost. When all chicks have been found, a new hen is chosen.

Halloween started more than 2,000 years ago. The Celts believed that the Prince of Darkness brought the cold and dark winter, and so they held a ceremony on this day to frighten away evil spirits that might be lurking about. The people dressed in frightening costumes to keep the spirits away. The tradition of bobbing for apples on Halloween comes from Pomona Day celebrations, when Romans set out apples and nuts in thanks for a good harvest. All Saints' Day, or All Hallows Eve, honors the saints. And in Ireland at this time, children carved out turnips to remember the folk tale of naughty Jack, who had to roam the earth with his lantern.

Paper Plate Masks

Materials:
White paper plates, elastic, stapler, mask patterns, crayons and markers, scissors, glue, colored yarn (optional)

Preparation:
Use the patterns for a guideline to cut a large section out of each plate for viewing—not simply two eyes, but a complete open area. Cut an appropriate length of elastic for each child and staple to the sides of their plate.

Activity:
Make several copies of each pattern and cut out. Let the children each choose a character and use markers or crayons to color in their mask. Have them glue the mask onto the plate. If desired, children can glue on yarn hair and whiskers.

Jack-o'-lantern Mask Pattern

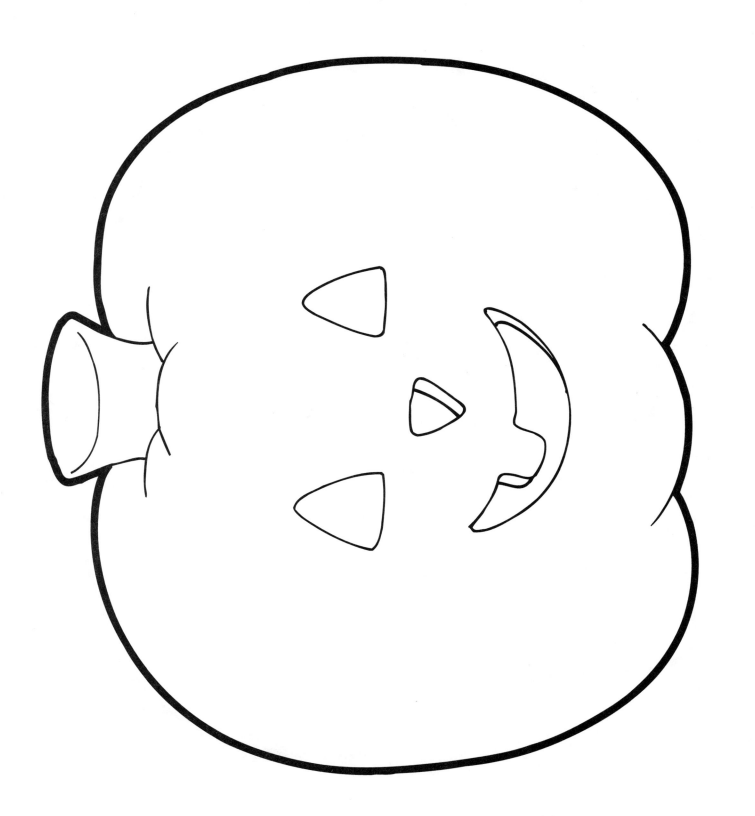

Cat Mask Pattern

Clown Mask Pattern

Spooky Cream Cheese Ghosts

Ingredients:
Celery sticks, soft cream cheese, sliced olives

Preparation:
Cut the celery pieces into sticks.

Treat:
Let the children spread the soft cream cheese into the celery sticks. They can add ghostly features with three sliced olives—two for wide eyes and one for a mouth!

Apple Pumpkins

Ingredients:
Large red or green apples (as round as possible); small, thin peeled carrots; raisins

Preparation:
Cut full, round slices of apple for each child. Carefully poke out any seeds. Cut thin rounds of carrots.

Treat:
Give each child a round apple slice. Let him or her add two carrot rounds for eyes, and poke raisins into the center for a mouth.

Try this:
There is an old superstition that says eating a crust of bread before going to bed on Halloween night makes your wish come true. Why not pass out nibbles of toast before naptime?

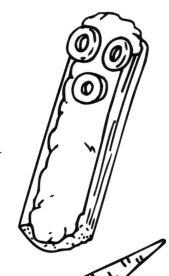

Some say that if a cat sits next to you on Halloween, you'll have good luck. If he sits in your lap, you'll have great luck! Find out with this fun game.

Cat-in-the-Lap Game

Materials:
Bean bag, black sock, white felt, safety pins, scissors, paper bag, slips of paper, marker, pumpkin container, small prizes such as erasers, stickers, pencils, nuts

Preparation:
To make the cat, place the bean bag in the sock and knot it. Cut triangle ears and a nose and two sets of whiskers from the white felt. Safety pin the features to the sock. Put the prizes in a pumpkin container. Write the numbers from 1 to 9 on slips of paper.

Activity:
Have the children sit in a circle with you. Pull out a numbered slip and show it. Pass the bean bag cat around to that number of children as the group counts—the cat sits next to the child it reaches on the final count. The child with the cat gets up and stands in place. Then pull out another slip of paper and show the number. The child with the cat walks that many steps as the group counts, then drops the cat in the lap of the person he or she comes to. That child then draws a prize from the pumpkin container and leaves the circle. Continue until each child has received a prize.

Trick or Treat?

Materials:
Candy corn, two baskets, slips of paper, marker

Preparation:
Write the word "trick" on a single slip of paper; write the word "treat" on another slip. Put both pieces of paper in a basket. On other slips of paper, write down different tricks such as: hop on one foot, close your eyes and touch your nose, roll over, balance on one foot, pat your head and rub your tummy, etc. Put all the tricks in the second basket.

Activity:
Let each child have a turn picking a piece of paper from the first basket. Choosing "treat" results in a piece of candy corn. Choosing "trick" results in reaching in to the second basket, performing the trick—and receiving two pieces of candy corn!

Did You Hear That?

Materials:
Sound effects aids, tape recorder and tape

Preparation:
Make a tape recording of some of the following spooky sounds: a creaky door, a dog howling, a cat screeching, a scream, some dramatic music, a faucet dripping, the wind blowing, thunder, ghoulish laughter.

Activity:
Play the sounds, one by one, and ask the children to identify each. If children are old enough, this is great fun in a slightly darkened room; it may be too much for little ones.

Try this:
Add a dose of reality to the spooky situation. Explain to the children how you made each recorded sound. You might also introduce a discussion of sound effects in movies or plays.

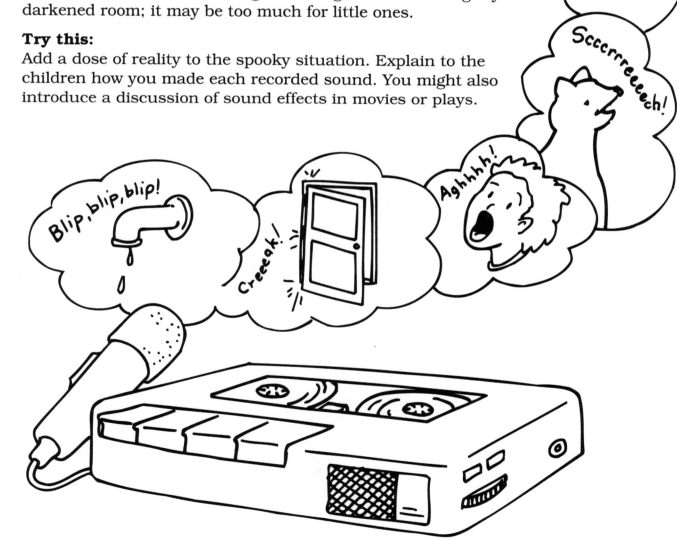

Halloween Pomander

Materials:
Large red apples, whole cloves, lengths of ribbon (cloth or the craft variety), bodkin or large needle, knife (optional)

Preparation:
For each pomander, knot one end of the ribbon, thread through the bodkin, and string through the apple core from bottom to top. (You may need to start the insertion hole with a knife.) Remove the bodkin and loop at the top for hanging.

Activity:
Show the children how to push the stem end of the whole cloves into the apple. They can make a mini jack-o'-lantern face by using several cloves to form eyes, nose, and mouth, or they can make random patterns. The children can take these sweet-smelling apples home to hang in the kitchen or on a doorknob.

Turnip Prints

Jack's lantern, as the story is told in Ireland, was really made from a turnip. Turnips are too small for little hands to carve, but why not let the class try making turnip prints?

Materials:
Turnips, sharp knife, several colors of tempera paint, pen, shallow dishes or pie tins, plain white paper

Preparation:
First slice each turnip in half through the middle. Outline a simple design on each half with the pen, such as a half moon, a star, a round cat face with ears, the features of a carved pumpkin, etc. Use the knife to carve away the surrounding turnip. Set out the turnips, pans of paints, and lots of paper.

Activity:
Let the children dip their turnips in the paint (remind them not to gather up too much paint) and then print a variety of designs on the white paper. Let the prints dry completely, then display.

Five Little Pumpkins Action Verse

Five little pumpkins (hold up five fingers)
Sitting on the fence (cross arms),
One fell off, and it rolled away.
(Flop out hand, then roll hands.)

Four little pumpkins (hold up four fingers)
Sitting on the fence (cross arms),
One fell off, and it rolled away.
(Flop out hand, then roll hands.)

Three little pumpkins (hold up three fingers)
Sitting on the fence (cross arms),
One fell off, and it rolled away.
(Flop out hand, then roll hands.)

Two little pumpkins (hold up two fingers)
Sitting on the fence (cross arms),
One fell off, and now it's pie!
(Flop out hand, rub tummy.)

One little pumpkin (hold up one finger)
Sitting on the fence (cross arms),
Now it's a jack-o'-lantern for you and I!
(Make a scary face, point to audience, then self.)

FAMILY DAYS
❖ Tango-no-sekku ❖

Tango-no-sekku is the traditional Boys' Day Festival in Japan, held in May. But both sexes should take part in making and enjoying these theme crafts. You can combine activities from Tango-no-sekku and Hina-matsuri (the traditional Japanese Girls' Doll Festival) to create a Children's Day celebration.

Flying Carp!

The carp represents courage, determination, and strength, fine qualities for both boys and girls to aspire to. In Japan, boys traditionally decorate their fish in black, and girls paint theirs red. But you may offer other colors as well.

Materials:
White butcher paper; carp pattern; long, thin plastic dowels or string; small, odd-shaped sponges; black and red paint; scissors; hole punch; binder hole reinforcements; shallow bowls

Preparation:
Cut large, simple carp shapes from the butcher paper, one for each child. On each fish, punch about three holes along the mouth end, press on the reinforcements, and then weave the dowel through. If dowels aren't available, simply attach string.

Activity:
Set out bowls of red and black paint and the sponges. Show the children how to dab on color to make a speckled, scale-like effect on their fish. When the carp are dry, they can be taken home and hung from eaves or doorways as colorful banners, or the dowels can be set in the ground in the school play yard to add to a Tango-no-sekku celebration.

Try this:
When making their flying fish, let the children write one letter of their name or their initials in each diamond shape across the carp, then color in.

Carp Pattern

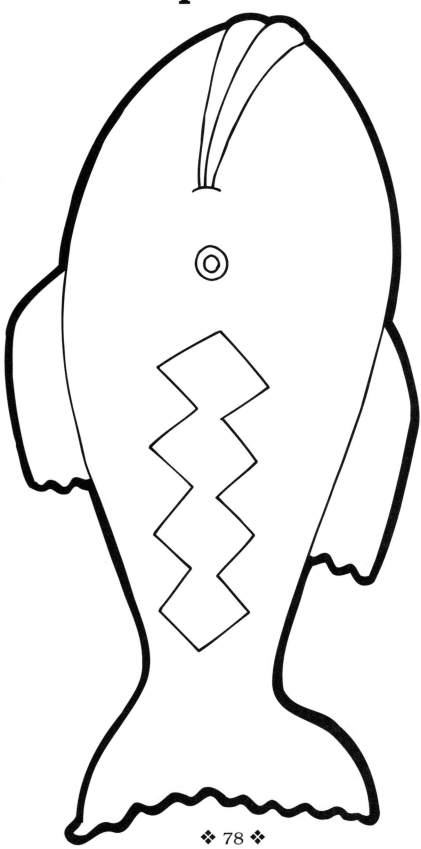

Tunnel Time

During this celebration in some parts of Japan, boys crawl through giant paper carps from head to tail for good luck. If you have a crawl-through tube, this makes a fun activity.

Materials:
Crawl-through tube, butcher paper, scissors, vinyl duct tape, markers or paint (optional)

Preparation:
Cut two large fish tail shapes and two rounded fish head shapes from the paper. If desired, draw in an eye and decorate the tail and head with markers. Attach the paper shapes to the ends of the tube with tape to make a giant carp.

Activity:
Give all the children a chance to crawl through the carp for good luck. Add to the fun by calling everyone wearing red shoes to crawl through the tube, then those wearing green socks, then those with five buttons, three pockets, eight shoelace holes, etc.

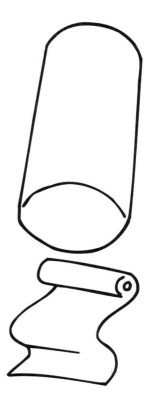

In March, Hina-matsuri, or the Girls' Doll Festival, is held in Japan. During the festival, special heirloom dolls are taken out of their boxes and displayed on a tiered platform of five to seven shelves. Peach blossoms, which represent sweetness, gentleness, and serenity (admirable qualities for both boys and girls), decorate the display.

Doll Display

Materials:
Small benches or boards and brick to create shelves; pink and white tissue paper; brown construction paper; scissors; glue; favorite dolls, teddy bears, or other stuffed animals the children bring from home

Preparation:
Cut each sheet of brown paper into a large branch shape and distribute. Cut the tissue paper into small squares.

Activity:
Allow the children to place their dolls and stuffed animals onto the shelves. Next, show the children how to crumple the tissue squares gently and glue them onto the brown branches for peach blossoms. Place the artwork around the doll display or tack on the walls.

Kodomo-no-hi, or Children's Day, is a modern Japanese national holiday held in May, celebrating children. Fruit-shaped candies, cake, rice, and sake are traditional treats for this special day. Here you'll find snack and activity ideas for this holiday; the ideas may also be used for a celebration that joins the Boys' Day Festival and the Girls' Doll Festival.

Children's Day Snack

Materials:
Fruit slices, whipped topping, cookies or crackers, milk or punch, food coloring

Preparation:
To make your party table colorful, let the children decorate paper cups with markers. And let them invite their favorite doll or snuggly animal to the table.

Treat:
Place portions of the whipped topping in several small bowls. Then add drops of food coloring to each (use the color chart for icings found on the bottle). Let the children count as you squeeze the drops, or let them add the drops themselves if they are able. The children can then dip pieces of fruit or cookies into the colorful toppings. Accompany the snacks with milk or punch.

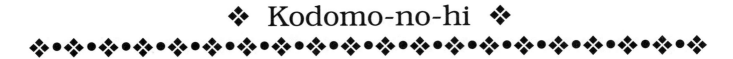

Baby Blanket Bonanza

Materials:
Have each child bring in a favorite baby blanket from home. (Most young children will still have a blanket, receiving cloth, or some type of "snuggly" to bring in.)

Activity:
Take time to let each child share his or her special blanket with the others. Some children may wish to tell who made the blanket or who gave it to them, or why the blanket is meaningful. Later, display the treasures by draping them over chairs or hanging them on the walls for the day.

Urini-nal is the name for Children's Day in Korea. This holiday, celebrated in May, is full of sports exhibitions, drum and dancing performances, and painting and creative writing contests. Tug of War is a favorite sport on this day, as well as a traditional rural contest in which children try to swing high enough to kick a bell hung on a pole.

Ring My Bell!

Materials:
Length of string, bell, swing set

Preparation:
Tie the bell to the end of a length of string.

Activity:
Stand away from a swing and hold the bell out high enough so that the children must swing high to reach it with a foot. Let each child swing until the bell has been kicked and rung.

Fan-tastic!

Materials:

Fan pattern, crayons or markers, scissors, small photo of each child, glitter, lengths of colorful ribbon, lightweight cardboard or heavy-duty construction paper, glue, hole punch

Preparation:

Cut out a fan pattern for each child. Glue the patterns to a cardboard or construction paper backing to make them sturdy. Punch a hole where indicated.

Activity:

Let the children color in the fan patterns and decorate with glitter if they choose. Show them the spot at the bottom of the fan for their picture, and let them glue it on. Then help them string colorful ribbon through the hole and tie it off. The children can carry their special fans on Children's Day or tack them to the wall for a colorful display.

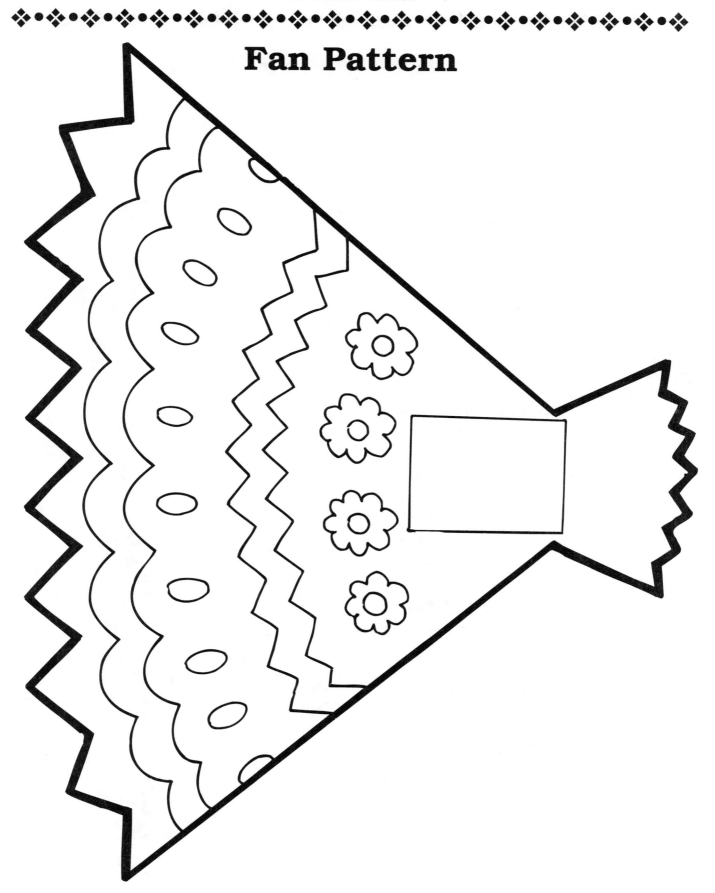

Fan Pattern

Kid Power Party Wear

Have the children start this day by wearing their most colorful clothing. They can add the following wristbands and crowns to remind them that they are courageous and powerful!

Power Bands and Courage Crowns

Materials:
Colorful metallic pipe cleaners, long strips of colored paper ribbon (ribbon in metallic finishes can be found at craft stores), child-sized plastic or metal bracelets (optional)

Preparation:
Shape and twist the pipe cleaners so that some fit around the children's heads and some slip on their wrists (or use the ready-made bracelets). Set out long lengths of colored ribbon.

Activity:
After the children have chosen a crown or wristband, show them how to attach the ribbon: fold the length of ribbon evenly in half, loop the folded end over the band or crown, and then slip the loose ends through the folded end. Encourage them to wear their finery with pride!

loop and pull

I'm Priceless!

Materials:

I'm Priceless! pattern, small photos of the children, colored construction paper, lightweight cardboard, pennies, glue

Preparation:

Copy enough patterns onto construction paper to give one to each child. Help the children glue their patterns to cardboard. Set out the pennies and glue.

Activity:

First have the children glue their picture to the top of the figure. Then have them count out the number of pennies they will need and glue one in each of the circles that outline the shape of the figure.

Try this:

Talk about the phrase "worth your weight in gold" and what it means. Then talk about the craft project and how each child is special, unique, and absolutely priceless!

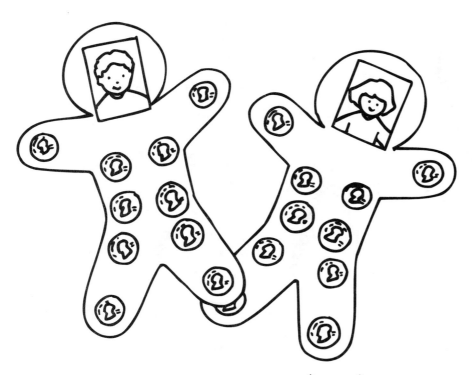

I'm Priceless! Pattern

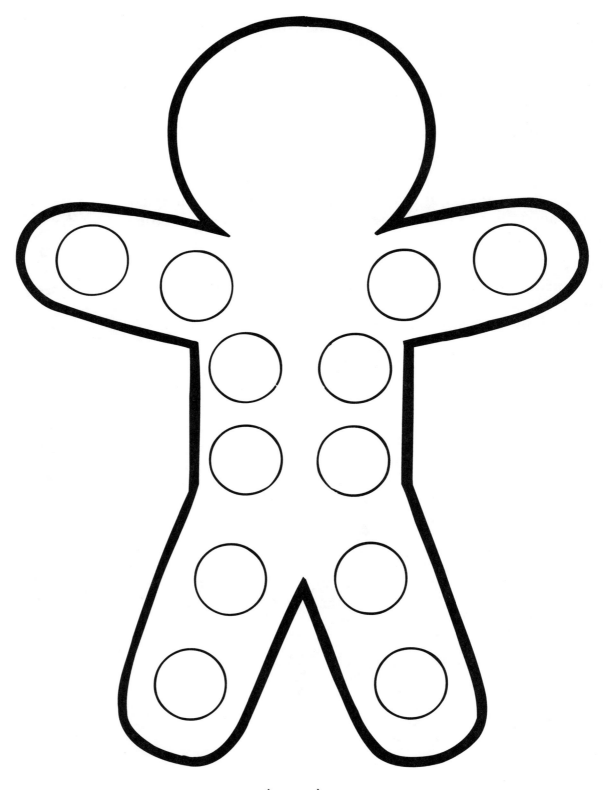

Little Star

(sing to the tune of "Twinkle, Twinkle, Little Star")

Sit in a circle and sing this song as a group. Let each child have a turn being the "star."

Twinkle, twinkle, little _____ ,
(Point to child named, who raises his or her hand.)
How we love just who you are!
(Hold hands to heart.)
Up above the world so high,
(Point to sky; child stands up.)
Like a diamond in the sky.
(Shake fingers like dazzling light.)
Twinkle, twinkle, little _____ ,
(Point to child, who takes a bow.)
How we love just who you are!
(Hold hands to heart; child sits down.)

Star Poems

Materials:
Star poem, colored construction paper, sequins and glitter, scissors, glue, yarn, hole punch, yarn, pencils or markers

Preparation:
Make copies of the star poem, one for each child, on colored paper. Cut out.

Activity:
Help the children write their name in the space provided on the poem. Then have them decorate the paper star with bright sequins and glitter. Make a hole in the top of the star and string with yarn to hang from the ceiling or doorway.

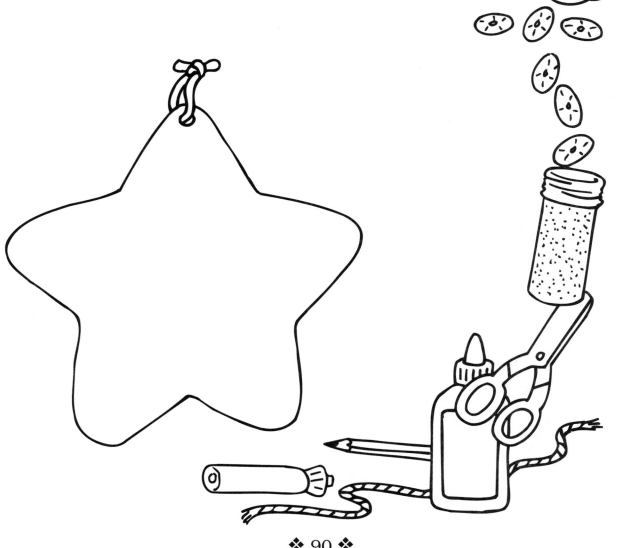

Little Star

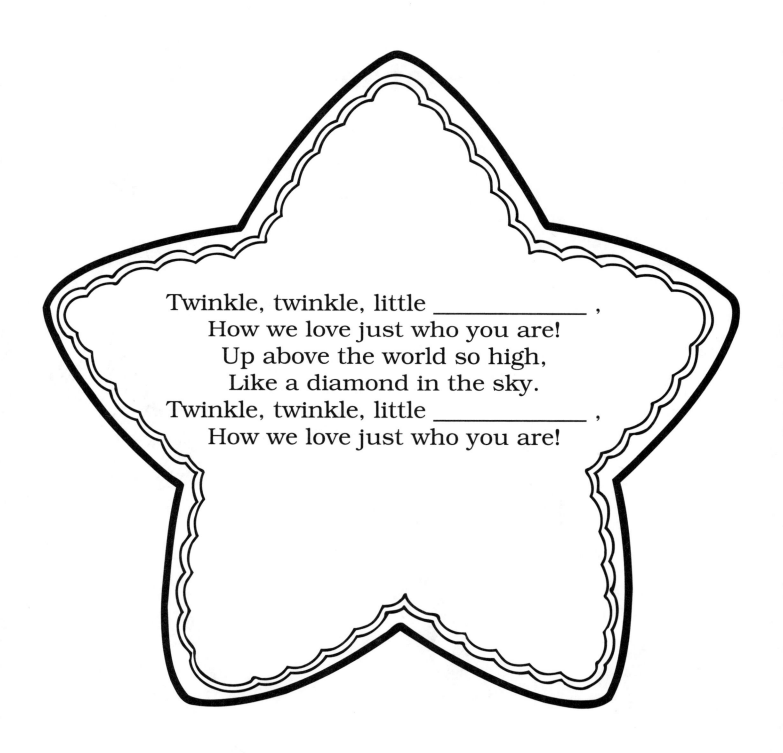

Twinkle, twinkle, little _____ ,
How we love just who you are!
Up above the world so high,
Like a diamond in the sky.
Twinkle, twinkle, little _____ ,
How we love just who you are!

New Year's Eve and New Year's Day are usually a time for late-night festivities and quiet hours spent in reflection on the past and coming year with the family. Following is a sampling of New Year traditions from around the world.

Shoogatsu—Japanese New Year

When the new year comes around, the Japanese like to tie red and white paper around brooms for good luck.

Materials:
Miniature straw brooms (available in craft stores) or Popsicle sticks and light brown paper to craft your own, red and white paper ribbons, glue, scissors

Preparation:
Give each child a mini broom or help the students make their own by gluing strips of brown paper onto the end of a Popsicle stick like broom bristles.

Activity:
Help the children tie or wrap several red and white ribbons around their broom. Hang the decorated brooms about the room for good luck.

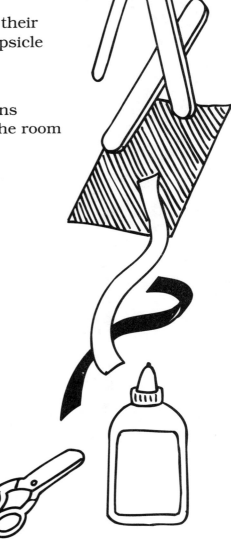

Chinese New Year

The parading dragon is a tradition at Chinese New Year, held in late winter. The children can create hand-held dragon decorations for a playful parade.

Materials:
White paper plates, dragon pattern, colored crepe paper streamers, markers or crayons, stapler, glue, scissors

Preparation:
Copy enough patterns to give one to each child. Cut the streamers into long lengths.

Activity:
Let the children color in their dragon pattern and then glue onto the paper plate. Help them to staple streamers all around the edges of the plate.

Dragon Pattern

Noche Vieja—Spanish New Year

In Spain and Portugal, bunches of grapes are both a tasty treat and a symbol of good fortune in the coming year. At midnight, one grape is eaten each time the clock strikes, to wish for good luck for each of the coming months of the year.

Ingredients:
Bunches of grapes

Treat:
Before letting the children enjoy their snack, talk with them about the meaning of the grapes for people celebrating the new year in different parts of the world. Then the children may serve themselves twelve grapes each. If you wish, have the children eat the grapes one by one, counting and calling out the name of each month as they go.

Happy New Year Action Verse

Make some noise!
(Shout with cupped hands.)
Stomp your feet, clap your hands!
(Stomp twice, clap twice.)
Shout "Happy New Year" across the land.
(Jump and circle arms about you.)
Make some noise!
(Shout with cupped hands.)
Blow a horn, bang a pan!
(Pretend to blow horn, clap hands like cymbals.)
Shout "Happy New Year" across the land.
(Jump and circle arms about you.)

Shout "Happy New Year" across the land.

Calendar Action Verse

January—Give a New Year's cheer!
(Jump up and cheer.)
February—Call your Valentine dear.
(Hold your hands to your heart.)
March—Is springtime near?
(Hand shading eyes, look about.)
April—Wet rain showers.
(Sprinkle fingers down.)
May—Bright new flowers.
(Hold hands together, burst fingers out.)
June—School is out!
(Jab thumb over your shoulder.)
July—Jump and shout!
(Leap and yell "yippee.")
August—Kick a beach ball.
(Give a kick.)
September—Brown leaves fall.
(Sprinkle fingers down.)
October—Goblins and ghouls.
(Make a scary face.)
November—Get out the harvest tools!
(Pretend to pick crop and place in basket.)
December—Snowballs fly.
(Pretend to throw snowball.)
January—It's another year—say goodbye!
(Wave goodbye.)

In the United States, Arbor Day is a day in April set aside to recognize the importance of protecting our national forests; trees are usually planted on this day. Recently, however, Earth Day, a more encompassing holiday, has been celebrated to remind people to protect all of our fragile environment.

Planters Parade

Materials:
Gardening tools such as small watering cans, rakes, and trowels; gardening wear such as sun hats, garden gloves, and bandanas; seedlings and soil

Preparation:
Prepare a parade route. Then have the children don gardening paraphernalia.

Activity:
Encourage the children to parade along the designated route. At the end of the parade, hold a planting party at which you plant a tree or have the children pot herb or flower seedlings.

Arbor Day "Tree-ts"

Ingredients:

Fruits and nuts, celery stalks, peanut butter or cream cheese, juice

Preparation:

Encourage the children to bring in any fruits or nuts growing on trees in their yards at home. Or ask them to go to the grocery store with a parent and choose a piece of fruit or several nuts that grow on trees. Arrange the fruits and nuts on a plate. Slice the celery stalks, leaving the leafy tops in place.

Treat:

Let the children help you spread cream cheese or peanut butter onto the leafy "mini trees." Serve the tasty trees along with juice poured into "tree-ts" cups (see below). As they munch the celery, fruits, and nuts, ask the children to name other foods that grow on trees.

Tree-ts cups:

Cover paper cups by taping strips of brown construction paper around them. Then let the children cut out and glue leafy green construction paper pieces all around.

Save the Planet—Recycle!

Materials:
Crates or cardboard boxes, poster board, markers

Preparation:
Talk about the importance of recycling. Prepare a flyer to parents describing your intention to collect aluminum cans and plastic bottles.

Activity:
Label two boxes or crates, one for aluminum and one for plastic. Encourage the children to bring in cans and plastic bottles and deposit them in the boxes daily. Create a chart on which you keep track of the number of cans and bottles collected each day. Let the children help in counting and marking the chart as contributions arrive. When you reach your target number, deliver the recyclables to a recycling center.

Earth Day Collage

Materials:
Butcher paper, magazines, scissors, glue, crayons or markers

Preparation:
Tack a large sheet of butcher paper low on the wall where the children can reach it. Label the top in bold letters, "We love (heart) our Earth." Mark off large sections and label them animals, birds, fish, flowers, forests, seas, etc.

Activity:
Encourage the children to find and cut out pictures of things that belong in each category. Then they can paste them on the butcher paper. This makes a great ongoing project—and the bigger the better!

Earth Day Song

(sing to the tune of "Miss Mary Mack, Mack, Mack")

Our little Earth, Earth, Earth (clap, clap, clap),
Keeps spinning round, round, round (spin finger round).
Through night and day, day, day (clap, clap, clap),
It's spinning round, round, round (spin finger around).

The trees so green, green, green (clap, clap, clap),
Need love and care, care, care (hug self, twist left and right).
So plant a tree, tree, tree (clap, clap, clap),
For all to share, share, share (clap, clap, clap).

The water so blue, blue, blue (clap, clap, clap),
Needs love and care, care, care (hug self, twist left and right).
It's up to you, you, you (point finger and shake),
To keep it there, there, there (clap, clap, clap).

The sky so bright, bright, bright (clap, clap, clap),
Needs love and care, care, care (hug self, twist left and right).
So keep it clean, clean, clean (clap, clap, clap),
Our wonderful air, air, air (clap, clap, clap).

Our little Earth, Earth, Earth (clap, clap, clap),
Keeps spinning round, round, round (spin finger round).
Through night and day, day, day (clap, clap, clap),
It's spinning round, round, round (spin finger around).

In many parts of Mexico, birthdays are traditionally family occasions, marked in a quiet way. A group of musicians may come to serenade the birthday boy or girl with a special song and then enjoy with the family hot chocolate and cookies baked in the shape of animals.

Hot Chocolate and Animal Cookies

Ingredients:
Instant chocolate mix, hot water or milk, plain animal-shaped cookies

Preparation:
Let the children help in measuring out the chocolate mix. Add the hot milk or water and stir.

Activity:
Let the children help themselves to the animal cookies and a cup of hot chocolate. Give everyone a turn to identify the animals they picked. As the children snack, ask them to name other animals. Also ask them to think about what type of animals might be found on a farm, at a circus, in the forest, or in the jungle.

Las Mañanitas—The Birthday Serenade

This is a popular song sung early in the morning to celebrate a birthday.

In Spanish:

Estas son las mañanitas,
Que cantaba el Rey David.
Y por ser el diá de tu Santo,
Te las cantamos a ti.

Despierta mi bien despierta,
Mira que ya amaneció.
Ya los pajarillos cantan,
La luna ya se metió.

In English:

This song is called "Las Mañanitas."
It was sung by King David.
Because it is your birthday,
We've come to sing it to you.

Arise, my dear, awaken,
See the sunrise of a new day.
The little birds are singing,
The moon has now gone away.

Feliz Cumpleaños Song

Uno, dos, tres,
Come to the birthday place!
(Wave people in.)
Quatro, cinco, seis.
Put on a birthday face!
(Draw a smile across face.)
One, two, three,
Fun for you and me!
(Point to audience, then self.)
Four, five, six,
Birthdays are a kick!
(Kick high.)

Birthday Menagerie

Materials:
Animal patterns, crayons, hole punch, yarn, coat hangers

Preparation:
Give each child one of each pattern.

Activity:
First let the children color in all the animals. When they're done, help them to make a hole, string with yarn, and suspend from the coat hangers.

Birthday Zoo Train

Materials:
Animal patterns, small shoe boxes, construction paper, glue, Popsicle sticks or strips of paper, crayons, hole punch, yarn

Preparation:
Help the children to cover their boxes with construction paper.

Activity:
Let the children color in their patterns and then glue them to the sides of their box. Show them how to glue on Popsicle sticks or paper strips, or they may simply draw on bars, spaced widely apart, all around the box like a cage. Connect the boxes with yarn to make a train.

Birthday Merry-Go-Round

Making this miniature merry-go-round is a fun group project.

Materials:
Large round pieces of Styrofoam, animal patterns, crayons, striped straws, artificial flowers, sequins, metallic cellophane, glue, tape

Preparation:
Copy enough patterns to give one of each to each child. Then help the children to decorate their round by gluing on flowers, sequins, crumpled cellophane, etc.

Activity:
Let the children color in their animal patterns and then tape each to a straw, with just a little of the straw extending from the top the way a merry-go-round pole would. They can poke a small artificial flower into the top of each straw for decoration. Then each child can poke the animals into the round, some farther down than others, to create the look of a merry-go-round with the animals going up and down.

Try this:
Talk to the children about their experiences on merry-go-rounds. Where were they? Have they ever seen one with animals other than horses? Extend this activity by playing some calliope music and letting the children dance around acting out the step and sounds of different animals—horses, rabbits, chickens, elephants, tigers, ostriches, and so on.

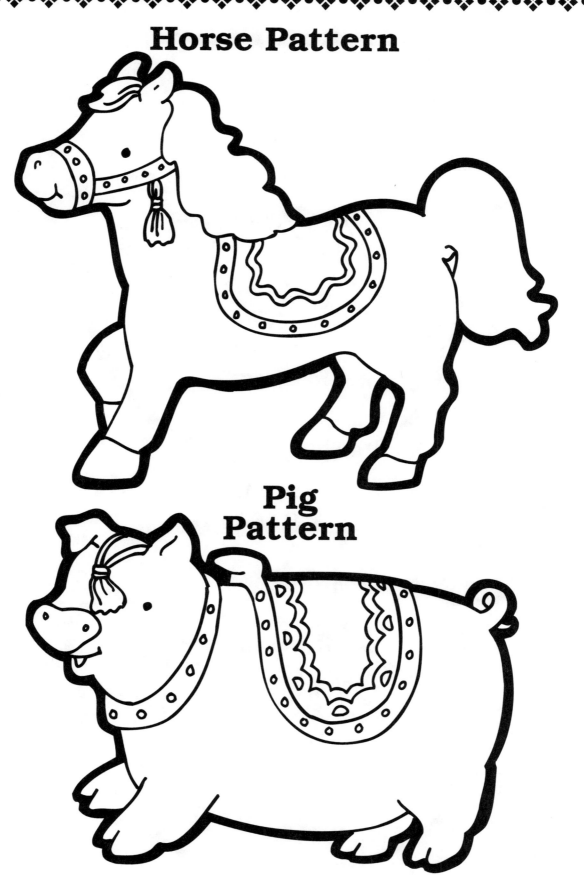

Horse Pattern

Pig
Pattern

Chicken Pattern

Duck
Pattern

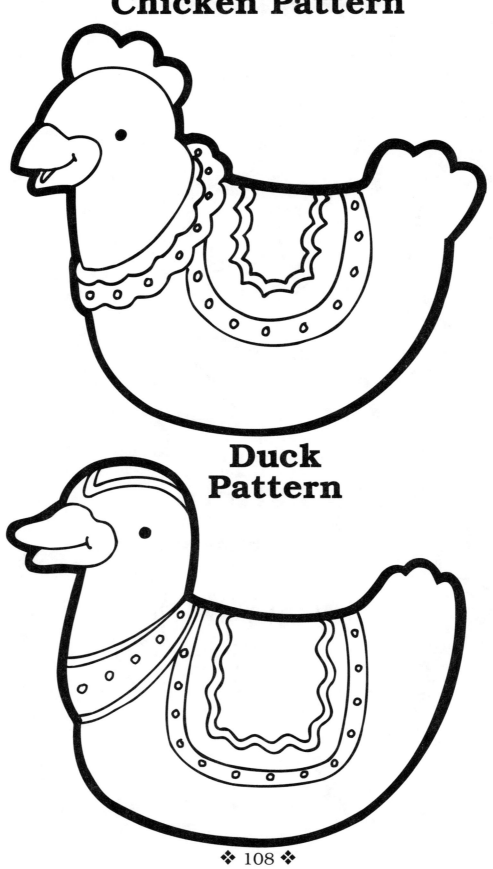

Tiger Pattern

Ostrich Pattern

Elephant Pattern

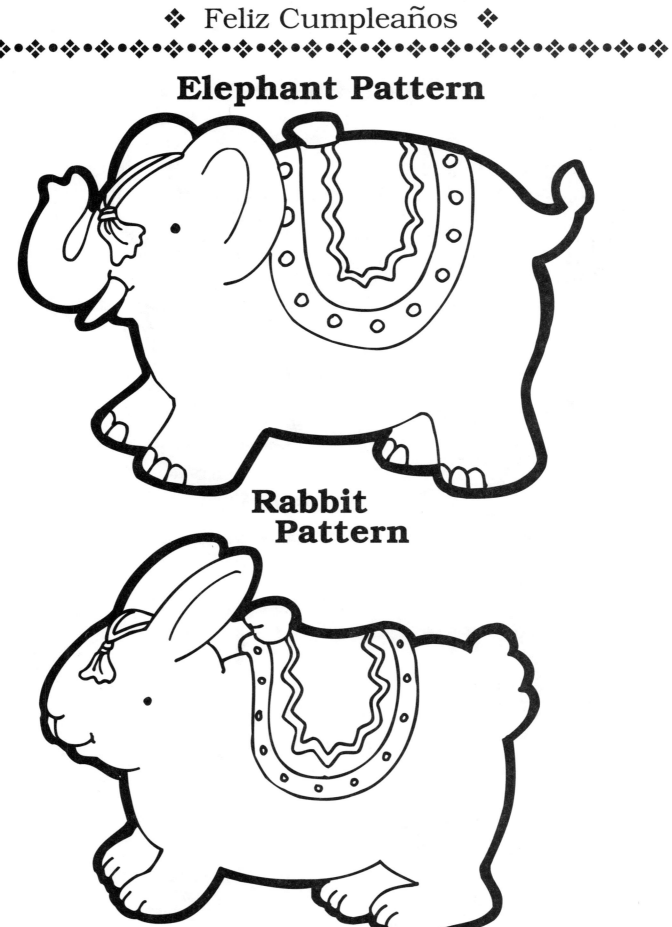

Rabbit Pattern

This Japanese summer festival day is set aside to remember ancestors. In the past, families would clean their homes, go to family graves to tend them, and set up a small altar in the home in respect for the deceased. They would also hang a white lantern in the doorway to light the way for their family members' spirits to come and share a meal. Today, O-bon is most known for the lantern boats that are set out to sail, representing departing spirits who had come to visit.

White Paper Lanterns

Materials:
Sheets of white construction paper, stickers (optional), glitter (optional), glue, Scotch tape, scissors, hole punch, yarn

Preparation:
Set out the materials. Be prepared to show the children how to fold their papers.

Activity:
Show the children how to place the paper in front of them, fold it evenly in half width-wise, and crease. Now they should open the paper, fold each side back into the middle, and crease. Finally, without cutting too far in, they should cut little triangles out of the folded edges. When they're done, they can open the folded paper and place the edges together while you tape them. Make two hole punches at the top, and string with yarn. Hang the lanterns across the room or in the doorway.

Try this:
Children who can't yet handle scissors can simply decorate their folded lanterns with stickers and glitter. Unfold in the same way, tape, and hang.

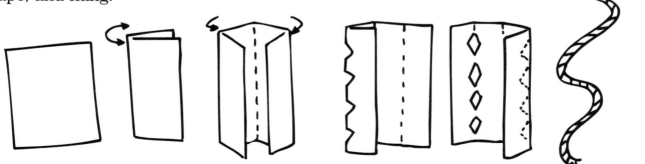

Lantern Boats

Materials:
Foam burger boxes (the notched kind that close securely), Popsicle sticks, cocktail straws, paper baking cups, glue

Preparation:
Make sure each child has a sturdy box. Set out the other materials.

Activity:
Show the children how to glue Popsicle sticks flat to the top of the box to create a wooden boat. (Make sure they leave a small space in the center to poke a straw through.) When the sticks have dried, help the children poke a straw through the center. Then help them take a cupcake liner (several stacked will be sturdier) and place it on the straw to represent the lantern. Float these little lantern boats in a puddle, plastic tub or wading pool, or a quiet stream or pond.

Diwali takes place near the end of October. This Hindu holiday is really a succession of several holidays one after another. A central focus is the lighting of dipas, little lamps that decorate the home and garden.

Dipas

Materials:
Colored clay, birthday candles

Preparation:
Prepare a work area.

Activity:
Explain to the children that during Diwali, dipas are placed along roofs, down garden paths, and along window ledges and balconies. Then have each child take a fistful of clay and shape a tiny saucer for a candle. Let the children gently press in a birthday candle and then line up their dipas in an appropriate place. Move the children to a safe area and then light the candles for a dazzling display.

Try this:
Ask the children to think of other times when light is a big part of a celebration (the birthday candles are a big hint for one occasion—but what are some others?).

Lakshmi's Swan

Dipas, or little lamps, are said to guide Lakshmi, a Hindu goddess of prosperity and fortune, to people's homes. Before the dipas are lit, people clean their homes and place wreaths of flowers on the door, then wait for Lakshmi's visit—a sign of prosperity for the coming year. Lakshmi is said to ride a swan or, some say, a heavenly owl.

Materials:
Swan patterns, white or brightly colored paper, jumbo cotton balls, glue and glitter mix, crayons, coins, glue, scissors, yarn, stapler, hole punch

Preparation:
Make a copy of each pattern piece for each child and cut them out. If the copies are made on white paper, the children can color in the details. If the undetailed side is copied onto bright solids, the children can decorate them with glitter. Fold one swan body together, staple it at the front, add the head, and staple again so the children will have an idea of what the finished swan will look like.

Activity:
Encourage the children to either color in the white swan pattern pieces or decorate the colored ones with glitter. When ready, help them assemble their swans. Then show the children how to shred the jumbo cotton balls and place them in the swan. Let them add a coin as a sign of the good fortune Lakshmi brings, then punch holes through the midsection and string with yarn to hang.

Try this:
Ask the children what other types of beings or objects they can think of that might symbolize good luck or prosperity—a leprechaun, a fairy, a shooting star?

Swan Pattern

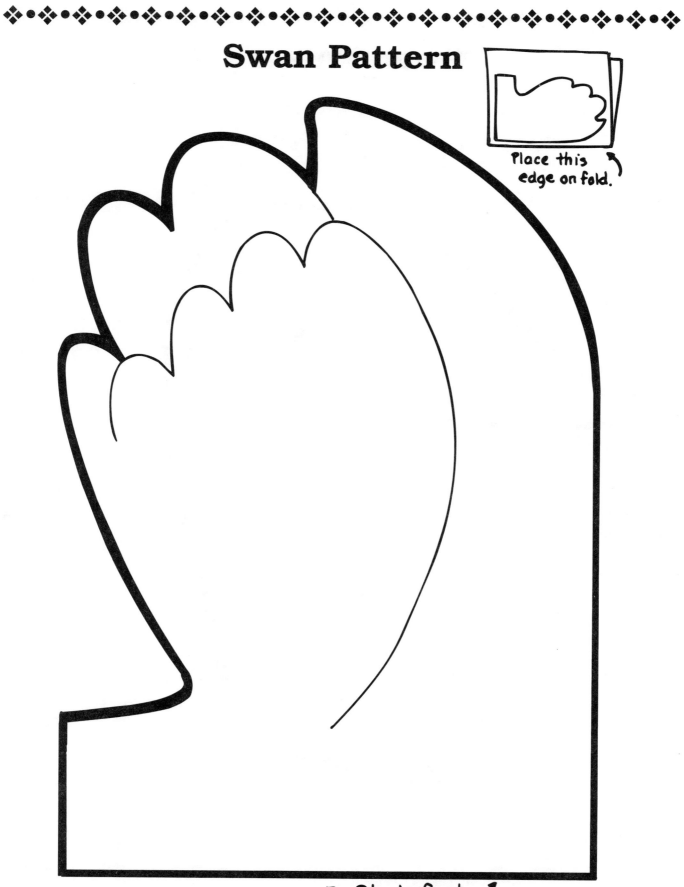

Place this edge on fold.

↖ Staple front. ↗

Swan Pattern

Alpanas

Aside from the glittering dipa lamps, observers of Diwali add beauty to their homes with alpanas—intricate good luck designs made on the ground near doorways with rice flour or powder. To create the designs, the rice flour is sifted through the fingers in a fine stream. Sometimes pigmented flour is added to the white outlines to add color. Alpanas picture birds, flowers, and intricate patterns.

Materials:
Rice flour or, if unavailable, white and colored chalk; or finger paints and white paper

Preparation:
For traditional alpanas, let the children practice sifting the rice flour through their fingers into a bowl so they can feel how to control the flow. Mark off a good-sized square for each child on a smooth pavement surface, preferably near a doorway. Or set out finger paints and a large piece of white paper for each child.

Activity:
Traditional: Let the children sift the flour through their fingers to make white designs on the pavement.
Chalk: Allow the children to create any design they wish within their square.
Finger paint: Let the children make large finger paintings to later lay on the ground to decorate the doorways.

For all types of alpanas, encourage the children to create birds and flowers, real or imagined, and other squiggly, curly designs.

Moon on a String

During Diwali, families gather to honor the moon—they prepare a feast and eat it under moon-shaped lamps. Here the children make paper moons they can sit under.

Materials:
Many different colors of paper in "moon colors"—pale yellow, white, even gray; thin lengths of metallic lightweight ribbon; small and large adhesive stars; flat sequins; scissors; glue; hole punch

Preparation:
Cut the paper into large circles. Distribute one round to each child.

Activity:
Show the children how to fan-fold the paper back and forth, then open it to give their moon dimension. Now let them press on stars or glue on sequins. Punch a hole in the top of each moon, and help the children string them with the thin, shiny ribbon. Hang the moons all about the room—let the children make several moons each if they wsh.

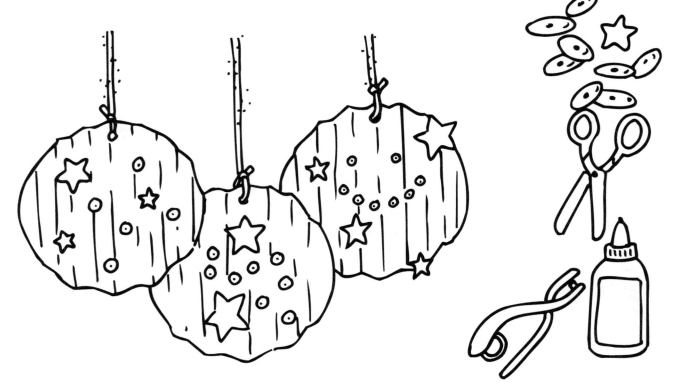

Moon Feast

People celebrating Diwali say the moon changes its face every fourteen days, so they share a meal of fourteen different dishes.

Ingredients:
Any favorite cold snack and finger foods

Preparation:
On the chalk board or a paper easel, list fourteen foods suitable to share in class. Let the children help in counting the items listed. You might even extend the activity by saying, "Count the number of fruits listed," "Count the number of sweets listed," etc.

Activity:
Assign each child a simple item to bring into class so that you end up with the necessary ingredients for the fourteen snacks. Hang paper moons, and share your meal beneath them!

Foods We Can Share in Class

apple
bananas
string beans
carrots
cookies
biscuits
cereal

crackers
grapes
popcorn
broccoli
cheese
jelly beans
oranges

Baskets of Love

Yama is the last Diwali holiday, in which brothers make promises of love and loyalty to their sisters. If a boy or man doesn't have a sister, he spends the day with a female cousin. Here the children make gifts that celebrate the love between brothers and sisters. Children who don't have a sibling can create their gift for a cousin or special friend.

Materials:
Strawberry baskets; shredded colored-paper confetti; small picture of each child and his or her sibling, cousin, or friend; colored paper; crayons or markers; scissors; treats such as popcorn, raisins, or nuts

Preparation:
On sheets of paper, write out the words "I love" and "I will" for each child. Go around the room and ask each child to name his or her sibling, and write the name in next to "I love." Next, ask the children what they might want to do for their brother or sister, and write that in under "I will." Encourage the children to choose simple things such as giving a hug. Cut out small heart shapes from different colors of paper.

Activity:
Give the children time to color in designs on the paper hearts. Have them place the hearts in their basket, then add some treats, the picture of themself and their sibling, and the written message, which has been folded up. Encourage the children to give this special gift with pride!

Kwanzaa is a time when African American families recognize traditional African harvest festivals; Kwanzaa means "first fruits." The celebration is also a time to stress the unity of the family. During Kwanzaa, a candle is set on a candle holder (a kimara) on a straw mat (a mkeka) in the middle of the table. The importance of lighting the candle is to remind people to work together, and to have pride in the family.

Mkeka

Materials:
Sheets of colored construction paper, uncooked (dry) linguine noodles, glue, scissors

Preparation:
Break the noodles in half. Cut each sheet of paper into four sections. Give a piece of paper to each child.

Activity:
Have the children spread liberal amounts of glue on one side of the paper. Then have them press on lengths of noodles so that they lay flat, covering the whole piece of paper to make it look like a straw mat. Let the mats dry completely. At home, candles may be placed on the mats.

Family Collage

Materials:
Extra-large sheets of red or pink paper, old magazines, family
photos, scissors, glue, marker

Preparation:
Cut large heart shapes from the paper and label the top of each
with a child's family name.

Activity:
Encourage the children to glue on pictures of their families. They
might also look through magazines for pictures to glue on that
relate to their families: the types of foods they eat, their favorite
TV shows, animals they like, or places in nature that they enjoy.

Zawadi

On the last day of Kwanzaa, gifts of love called zawadi are given. Help the children create a variety of little gifts to share with family members.

Materials:

A variety of packaging materials—empty matchboxes, toilet paper tubes, frozen-juice containers, small plastic tubs with lids, empty spice jars, etc.; decorations such as construction paper, tissue paper, stickers, glitter, etc.; glue; tape; scissors; gifts or treats such as small photos, paper cutouts or snowflakes, crayon drawings or clay creations, stickers, erasers, nuts, raisins, candy

Preparation:

Clean or prepare the containers. Tape closed one end of any open tubes. Distribute the containers and set out the decorating materials.

Activity:

Ask the children to decorate their containers with any of the colorful materials. Then allow them to create a special drawing or other gift (see above) and place it in the container. Help the children secure their zawadi and encourage them to give the gifts to loved ones.

Note:

Traditional Kwanzaa treats include peanut brittle, pecan pralines, sweet potato and marshmallow pudding, and fruit.

This eight-day Jewish celebration of an historical battle for religious freedom occurs in December. The Feast of Lights, or Hanukkah, is a joyous holiday marked by the lighting of the candles in the menorah, a nine-branch candelabrum. One candle is lit each day for eight successive days; the ninth candle is used to light the others.

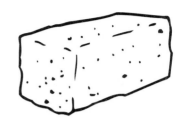

Floral Menorah

Materials:
Florist's oases (the green material used for flower arrangements); fresh or dried flowers, pods, seeds, leaves, etc.; birthday candles; knife; small aluminum tins; water

Preparation:
Take a walk with the children to collect flowers and other natural materials. Cut the stems to short, sturdy spikes. Cut off a good-sized rectangular section of oasis for each child. Wet each oasis and set it in a small aluminum tin.

Activity:
First have the children cover their oasis by pressing in some flowers, leaves, grasses, etc. When their bricks are covered, they can gently press in eight candles all in a row. Have them place a ninth candle in the center, a little bit forward of the line.

Note:
This makes a nice group project if a large oasis and large candles are used.

Sing a Song of Hanukkah

(sing to the tune of "Sing a Song of Sixpence")

Let the children know that a dreidel is a special four-sided top
used in games at Hanukkah.

Sing a song of Hanukkah, a pocketful of light.
Spin the dreidel, do a dance, light the candles bright.
When it's time for Hanukkah, we all begin to sing!
Isn't the menorah light such a pretty thing?

People Gather 'Round Action Verse

People, people, gather 'round,
(Arm out to left, then right, then wave in.)
Bring your lantern,
(Hold up imaginary lantern.)
Sound the gong!
(Clap hands together.)

Lights are shining all around,
(Spin around.)
Twinkling, twinkling,
(Make little bursts with fingers.)
All night long!
(Make grand swoop with arms.)

Light the Candle

(sing to the tune of "Row, Row, Row Your Boat")

Light, light, light the candle
Glowing in the night.
Merrily, merrily, merrily, merrily,
Candles burning bright!

Friends, friends, gather 'round
On this family night,
Merrily, merrily, merrily, merrily,
Candles burning bright!

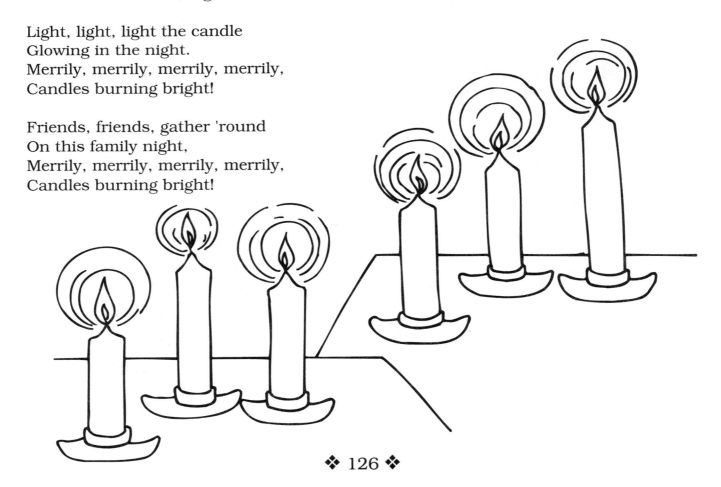

RESOURCES

Holiday Resources

Beaton, Clara. *The Complete Book of Children's Parties.* New York: Kingfisher Books, 1991. (all-year activities)

Darling, Kathy. *Holiday Hoopla: Flannel Board Fun.* Palo Alto, CA: Monday Morning Books, 1990.

Darling, Kathy. *Holiday Hoopla: Multicultural Folk Tales.* Palo Alto, CA: Monday Morning Books, 1994.

Darling, Kathy. *Holiday Hoopla: Plays, Parades, Parties.* Palo Alto, CA: Monday Morning Books, 1990.

Jones, Anita W. *Door to Chinese Festivals, Feasts, Fortunes.* Taiwan: Mei Ya Publications, 1971.

Kroll, Steven. *Oh, What a Thanksgiving!* New York: Scholastic, 1988.

Nabwire, Constance and Bertha, Vining. *Cooking the African Way.* Minneapolis: Lerner Publications, 1988.

Rice, Melanie. *The Complete Book of Children's Activities.* New York: Kingfisher Books, 1985. (all-year activities)

Rockwell, Anne. *A Bear Child's Book of Special Days.* New York: E. P. Dutton, 1989.

Suid, Anna. *Holiday Crafts.* Palo Alto, CA: Monday Morning Books, 1985.

Song and Poem Resources

Burgie, Irving. *Caribbean Carnival: Songs of the West Indies.* New York: Tambourine Books, 1992.

Hopkins, Lee Bennett. *Ring Out—Wild Bells.* New York: Harcourt, Brace, Jovanovich, 1992. (holiday and seasonal poems)

Slier, Deborah. *Make a Joyful Sound: Poems for Children by African-American Poets.* New York: Checkerboard Press, 1991. (songs and poems)

Picture Books to Share

Feelings, Muriel. *Moja Means One: A Swahili Counting Book*. New York: Dial, 1976. (Kwanzaa)

Hirschi, Ron. *Seya's Song*. Seattle: Sasquatch Books, 1992. (Salmon Harvest)

Nerlove, Miriam. *Hanukkah*. New York: Albert Whitman, 1989. (Hanukkah)

Prelutsky, Jack. *It's Halloween*. New York: Scholastic, 1977. (Halloween)

Tompert, Ann. *Bamboo Hats and a Rice Cake*. New York: Crown, 1993. (Japanese New Year)

Waters, Kate and Madeline Slovenz-Law. *Lion Dancer, Ernie Wan's Chinese New Year*. New York: Scholastic, 1990. (Chinese New Year)

Winter, Jeanette. *Follow the Drinking Gourd*. New York: Dragonfly Books, 1988. (African-American history)

Folk Tale Picture Books

Aardema, Verna. *Bringing the Rain to Kapiti Plain*. New York: Dial, 1983. (African)

Ata, Te. Adapted by Lynn Moroney. *Baby Rattlesnake*. San Francisco: Children's Book Press, 1989. (Native American)

Bishop, Claire Huchet and Kurt Wiese. *The Five Chinese Brothers*. New York: Sandcastle Books, 1989. (Chinese)

Cole, Joanna. *Best-loved Folktales of the World*. New York: Doubleday, 1982. (International)

Czernecki, Ed and Timothy Rhodes. *The Sleeping Bread*. New York: Hyperion, 1992. (Guatemalan)

Ginsburg, Mirra. *The Chinese Mirror*. New York: Harcourt, Brace, Jovanovich, 1988. (Chinese)

Mayo, Margaret. *Magical Tales from Many Lands*. New York: Dutton's Children's Books, 1992. (International)

McDermott, Gerald. *Zomo the Rabbit: A Trickster Tale from West Africa*. New York: Harcourt, Brace, Jovanovich, 1992. (West African)

Mosel, Arlene. *Tikki Tikki Tembo*. New York: Holt, 1992. (Chinese)

Retan, Walter. *Favorite Tales from Many Lands*. New York: Grosset and Dunlap, 1989. (International)